Walk *the* WALK
(And stop talking the TALK)

BY

OLAWUNMI BIRIYOK

Walk the Walk
. . . and stop talking the talk
by Olawunmi Biriyok

Printed in the United States of America

ISBN 9781625096005

Unless otherwise indicated, Bible quotations are taken from the King James Version.

www.xulonpress.com

TABLE OF CONTENTS

DEDICATION

*I*n all things, we give God the glory so; first and foremost, I wish to dedicate this book to the three most
important persons in my life: God the Father, God the Son
and God the Holy Spirit for the knowledge, inspiration and
strength given to me throughout my writing of this book.

I also want to dedicate this book to the blessed memory
of my late father, Chief Taiye Shonowo, fondly remembered
as Olla Balm, for being a lovely and respected earthly father
to me, May your gentle soul rest in eternal peace with the
Lord. My sweet mother, Mrs Phebean Shonowo, fondly
called Sisi, my husband, Casimir Biriyok and my children,
Naomi, Nufi, Nasara and Zachariah for being there for me

and knowing that I can always count on your support and patience.

To my special trusted friends, Dr Koku Adomdza who contributed immensely by utilising his valuable time to proofread and with his constant promptings to urge me on, not forgetting Dr Anato Dumelo who continuously supports and encourages me and to Betty Croffie, Ajike Ajala, Perpetua Abban and Iris Asare my dear sisters in the Lord who have always stood by me, invested their time and resources and taken keen interest in what I do. To all my siblings, I love you all and special thanks to Olabosipo Osude for her demonstrated support. My numerous nephews and nieces, God bless you all. Mario Croffie, I appreciate you in the Lord. My brothers and sisters in the Lord, especially, the team of Joy and Company and my publishers, Xulon Press, I sincerely thank you all for your support, friendship and encouragement. May Almighty God graciously bless you!

PREFACE

Dear Reader,

Walking the Walk and not just talking the talk means practising and actualising the Word and not just speaking words inconsistent with the Word of Life. This book is pregnant with practical experiences and testimonies to inspire you to the extent of provoking divine anointing to the glory of God.

Taking in all the recent scenes of life – the troubles, despair from the causes and effects and aftermaths of escalated global calamities such as hurricanes, earthquakes, floods and terrorism, not to exclude the unprecedented global recession –you will come to realise in the ensuing chapters that hope and peace are assured to all when in deep distress to Him we call and to our rescue He surely comes.

In this book, I want to teach and share the simple practical ways of being and continuing to be in tune with God. Whatever your religious background, Christians and non-Christians alike, you will be blessed by this book, as it brings home truth, hope and faith in Christ Jesus. Remember that Christ came and lives for all – sinners and the righteous alike! This is therefore a must read book that will transform your life, to God's glory.

Throughout the contents of this awe-inspiring book, I will share some life experiences with you, that will be an eye opener to the simple ways of living a Christian lifestyle on a daily basis. Be ready, fasten your seat belt and enjoy the transition from the ordinary walk of Christian life to supernatural manifestations of God's grace, uncommon favours and miracles, in your discovery of an extraordinary walk in divine honour with God.

Join me as we embark on the long-awaited journey of a lifetime! It's a privilege to have you on board!

Olawunmi Biriyok

INTRODUCTION

*T*his inspirational book in your hand, though it may appear little, will reveal the intrinsic values of the ordinary Christian journey, to an extraordinary destination in Christian life. It depicts our relationship with God – which is, one of a covenant.

Our walk in life revolves around our covenant relationship with God. By this, I mean, the biblical compact between God and the whole world (1 John 2:2). To this end, it will include both Christians and non-Christians. Therefore if we want to live a life that accords with God's grace and will for us, we must stop talking about knowing what to do, and actually fall in line, and walk the walk of righteousness that embodies **faith, humility, obedience, selflessness, love, gratitude and prayers.** The one million-dollar question on everyone's lips, I presume is, how do I do this? Simple! - is my answer to this enquiry and the method is explained in the next few paragraphs.

Firstly, is to walk the Walk in **Faith**. By this I mean to develop an attitude of expectancy in all circumstances of your life rather than focusing on the negatives. We must be faithful to God from the start of our walk with Him, to the very end of ages. That is to say, to operate in faith through our entire lives.

Secondly, is to walk the Walk in **Humility**. We can do this by humbling ourselves in the sight of the Lord, and having proper respect for God when we call on Him, to take away our sinful pride. This entails us comparing ourselves only with Jesus Christ, to realistically assess our sinful nature and commitment to serve; as we ought to do. Thereby using our God given gifts as Christ directs, to the glory of our Almighty Father.

Thirdly, is to walk the Walk in **Obedience**. This is done, by trusting and following God by faith. We need to cultivate an attitude to wholly rely - without reservations or doubts - on God. Knowing and respecting the fact that, our true freedom comes from obedience to God's words, enabling us to distinguish right from wrong. This way, we do not use our liberty to indulge in sinful nature but to serve one another in love.

Fourthly, is to walk the Walk in a **selfless** manner, disregarding ourselves or our own interests, to take up the command and challenge to trusting in our God wholeheartedly with our souls, bodies and minds and to love our neighbours as ourselves. When we adopt and practice sacrificial love, by being there for one another, we ensure that our daily lifestyles mirror the command of God.

Fifthly, is to walk the Walk in **Love**. "Love is patient, love is kind. It does not envy, it does not boast, it is not proud. It is not rude, it is not self-seeking, it is not easily angered, it keeps no record of wrongs. Love does not delight in evil but rejoices with the truth. It always protects, always trusts, always hopes, always perseveres. Love never fails" (1 Cor. 13:4-8). This priceless gift of all ages, must be accepted as a gift from God, then and only then, will you be in the position to share it with God's creation as provided in the walk with God. Love as we all know, is so amazing and so divine. We thus, need to strive in our walk of love, to make the gift of love in each one of us, a true reflection of the perfect love that comes from God above.

Sixthly, is to walk the Walk in **Gratitude**. We are called to "give thanks in all circumstances, for this is God's will for us in Christ Jesus" (1Thess. 5:18). Whether we are in good or bad circumstances, we must be thankful in every-thing for God's presence and the good that He accomplishes in such unpleasantness. The need to cultivate an attitude of gratitude on a daily basis is paramount. It thus goes without saying that, in our walk of gratitude, we have to include in our "must-do" list; a daily expression of our thanks to God and to mankind for their assistance and blessing in our lives.

Lastly, but not the least, is to walk the Walk in and with ceaseless **Prayers**. Just as Jesus Christ told His disciples a parable to show them how to always persist in prayer without giving up, we also need to, with full concentration, constantly keep our requests before God as we walk daily with Him, without giving up.

The good news is that, everyone sincerely willing to walk the Walk, can. Yes, you can! I am no different from you but yes, I am walking the Walk with absolutely no regrets. Walking the Walk is not limited to any race or group. For sal-vation is offered to all; no matter what your colour, nation-ality, creed or language is. God is inviting you now. Are you ready to walk the Walk with Him? If you are, Read On!

ONE

LEARNING TO WALK THE WALK

"How can a young man keep his ways pure? By living according to your word. I seek you with all my heart do not let me stray from your commands." Ps.119:9-10.

*T*aking the first step of a journey of a lifetime, is no easy task, in the e midst of fear, despair, disappointments, failures, you name it, but the promises of God make it worthwhile. Just as a child learns to walk by experience – falling down many a time and picking itself up, so do we have to learn to walk with God, though we may fall. As with a child, we must pick ourselves up no matter what and continue in our walk. For if we resolve not to learn to walk, because of trials and sufferings, we will never learn to walk. All it takes, is courage and willpower, to take that very first step of the walk with God. No doubt we must, first and foremost, purge ourselves from all unrighteousness and begin to trust in Christ. This is what I describe as being the first step to turning to God, when we are bold enough to say to the rest of the world, "I don't care what anybody says or thinks of me but I am doing an about-face – 180-degree turn – from the kind of self-centeredness that leads to wrong actions and to admit my sin". For the word of God says. "Repent for the Kingdom of heaven is near" (Matt. 3:1-2).

What one sees these days is this; many people are yearning to benefit from a close relationship with Jesus Christ without shunning sin or admitting their disobedience to the Word of God. Unfortunately, we cannot walk the walk with Him, without responding to God's call to us to repent so our sins may be blotted out. The key to repentance in the walk with our Maker is confessing our ungodly ways and wholly turning to Him in obedience.

When we do this, God receives us and cleanses us of our sins. It is only God that can get rid of our sins and help us live the way He wants us to.

When we exchange our sin for His righteousness, so that His righteousness is poured into us at our conversion, God in His infinite mercy, offers to trade, Christ's righteousness for our sins. Glory!

Seeking God often appears to be rough and tumble, because that journey of life, is met with so many trials and tribulations, to the extent that the very relationship you are building with God may get worse before it gets better. Trials are always awaiting us and we may be shocked by circumstances facing us, but God is never surprised because before we were born, He knew us. The Author of our destiny is readily available, if only we will sincerely cleanse ourselves and turn to His ways.

The truth of the matter is, you are on the right path to attaining a spiritual milestone, to the disappointment of many others, - be it friends, family members or acquaintances - but to the approval of the Most High God, whose ultimate opinion of you, matters. This is exactly what God wants of us, the very essence of walking and living righteously with Him. We are told in Hosea 10:12

"Sow righteousness for yourselves,
reap the fruit of unfailing love,
and break up your unplowed ground;
for it is time to seek the LORD,

17

until he comes

and showers his righteousness on you."

Be encouraged by the fact that, in the book of Genesis we are told that, the devil, called Satan, tempted Eve in the Garden of Eden and, in the book of Matthew 4, even tempted Jesus Christ in the desert. Sight should not be lost of the fact that Satan is a fallen angel; he is real and not symbolic, and is constantly fighting against people like you and me, who have resolved to, take the first step to, begin the walk of Christian life, to follow and obey God.

There is no doubt in my mind that, to truly know God and begin to enjoy the vast blessings He has in store for us, we must come to repentance, turning away from sin. The joy of repentance is, not only does it humble us in the sight of God to receive forgiveness, but it helps us see ourselves, including our sin, more clearly. As we see our sin, we must repeat the process of repentance to constantly fellowship with God. When we seek God first with all our hearts and make Him the centre of our lives, He will provide for *all* our needs and beyond.

Once we are in a relationship with God, paramount knowledge of the bare essentials of that relationship is required, in order to be able to both understand and nurture it. Here, I am talking about the covenant relationship with God, where God promises divine blessings if we walk with Him in His word. The history of this biblical form of relationship stems from God's covenant with Noah and Abraham.

What then is a covenant? A covenant is a promise. God made promises with His people so that, although God was going to destroy the world by flood, due to Noah's righteousness, God spared Noah and his family's lives; by instructing Noah to build an ark of cypress wood and to take inside the ark certain animals and told him, *"I will establish my covenant with you"* (Gen 6:18). And with Abraham, God instructed him to get out of his country, and his father's house, to a land that He would show him and said *"I will make you a great nation; I will bless you and make your name great"* (Gen. 12:1-2). He promised to give Abraham the land of Canaan in Genesis 15. These covenants are discussed fully in chapter three below. Suffice it to say, the covenants, as we see, were made between a superior party, God, and inferior party, Noah/ Abraham (man) both of whom were not in any position to bargain or haggle over the terms of the promises.

Note that the Lord did not set any conditions for man to observe *except* to obey His instructions. How reassuring it is to know God's covenant is established with us. He is faithful to keep to His word and would thus keep us safe through our relationship with Him. What are His instructions, one may ask? And how are they applicable to us today?

WHAT ARE HIS INSTRUCTIONS?

"To seek first His kingdom and His righteousness . . ." (Matt. 6:33). This is the holiness of heart and purity of life, which God requires of those who profess to be subjects of His spiritual kingdom. Our salvation ought to engross us entirely as we are called to turn to God first for help, filling our thoughts with His desires, giving Him the first place in every area of our lives and indeed taking His character for our pattern and to serve and obey Him in everything. This calls for a repentant heart, which is a change of mind, direction or will - that is produced by godly sorrow and the goodness of God - that results in a turn around or reformation of life.

This is done when we confess our sins and accept Jesus Christ as our Lord and Saviour. Otherwise we will die in our sins, if we reject the only way to be rescued from sin. Many people out there in the society you and I live in have

20

sadly, turned blind eyes to this priceless gift of life and deaf ears to the precious call to, walk the walk of divine honour and righteousness. They have contrarily, chosen to take the ungraceful path that leads to destruction and condemnation. Repent! and receive Jesus Christ's gift of amazing love. Make Him your Lord and Saviour, is the call today; don't miss out on it!

AND HOW ARE THEY APPLICABLE TO US TODAY?

The continuation of the verse above promises us that *". . .and all these things will be given to you as well."* Our natural goals and worldly desires, all compete for priority but we are promised the free bounty of whatever need that we ask of God. We receive these blessings because of the goodness, mercy and liberality of God, without our thought and care, and much less merit, except by His special grace.

We must, however, be strategically positioned to receive all of these promised blessings. It only takes a courageous first step of repentance to launch into righteousness. God's promises are by no means empty promises. He commands us to seek first His kingdom and His righteousness; and take good note of what He says: that "all these things will be given to you as well." This is His invitation to all of us, to seek eternal life. We, on our part, can accept this divine invitation, and be saved – if we confess with our mouth, "Jesus is Lord" and by believing that Jesus Christ died for our sins, was buried, and rose again on the third day.

Therefore, if anyone is in Christ he is born again, a new creation; the old has gone, the new has come and the Lord Jesus Christ will help you to walk uprightly in righteousness.

Surrendering all to God is the key. For the Spirit of God, the Holy Spirit, to begin to dwell, work and manifest in our lives, we must in the first instance, give it all up for Christ. Now, there are no two ways about it. When you heed to the call to walk the Christian walk, you will be overwhelmed with the zeal to gladly confess, without inhibitions, with your mouth that Jesus Christ is Lord and believe in your heart that God raised Him from the death, so you are saved. For it is with your heart that you believe and are justified, and it is with your mouth that you profess your faith and are saved. As Scripture says, "Anyone who believes in Him will never be put to shame." Romans 10.

Let me share my experience of this with you, my "Boston Experience" as I term it. In the summer of 1987 whilst visiting my nephew and some friends in Boston, Mas-

sachusetts in the United States of America, I went to one of
their shopping malls in Framingham and while going about
my business looking for bargains in shops, a pretty lady
approached me. There was something strikingly attractive
about her and I wondered what she wanted with me. Her
aura and heart-melting smile froze my being and I had no
choice but to hear her out. Pleasantries were exchanged with
this "stranger" who, after carefully thinking out her choice
of words, asked me if I was walking with the Lord. This
unexpected one million dollar question threw me off guard,
calling for my thinking cap. Instead, my initial reaction was
that of a typical rebel: I swiftly shifted into the defensive
mode and wondered, how dare she ask me this question.
Realising my hesitation, she went on to share the Word with
me, in a most appreciated subtle manner and, invited me to
her flat or as it is commonly referred to in America, her con-
dominium, for dinner.

I believe it was my time for the call from God to walk
with Him by actualising His word, because not before long, I
was seated in this stranger's house with her fellow Christian
flatmates. They received me warmly and we chatted casu-
ally over dinner, nothing overbearing, just a light-hearted
conversation, taking turns to each share their testimonies of

their first love for Christ. The meal I had that night was no ordinary meal, it was a fabulous meal wrapped in a lively conversation, that I call "the repentance meal." The path of my life was never to be the same again from thereon.

Sharon Pickering, as I came to know her name, paved the way, setting me in the right direction of my walk. She ignited in me, unprecedented fire for the love of Christ. Of course, she would not know that as a result of her boldness in witnessing to me, I gave my life to Christ in the spring of the following year. Two of her resounding words, were that Jesus Christ loves me and I was to repent of my sins. She left me with the gift of a Bible.

I am not one usually dissuaded by turbulence when travelling by air; on the contrary, I love the rollercoaster feeling of the churns in my stomach. My flight back to England, United Kingdom, was very turbulent and, believe you me, on this particular occasion, was least enjoyable. I did not perceive the fun this time around, except, it was filled with fear and regret. Thus, with my eyes closed and glistening tears trickling down my face, I held the Bible Sharon had given me, in my hand clutched to my bosom and said to God, "You know I have searched myself and found that I do not know you as I ought to. I have decided to surrender my life to you, so do not let this aeroplane crash until I have been baptised." On arrival, I immediately contacted the UK branch of Sharon's church to be baptised and on 22nd March 1988 I became a new creature to the glory of God.

Today, the knock-on effect of my Boston Experience spans years of my walk in the goodness and mercy of God. The benefits of this honourable walk surpass the liabilities, which are, stepping stones to disguised benefits. You too can experience this; only if you will heed the call. Like me, is a "stranger" trying to point *you* in the right direction by way of sharing the bible contents with you? Or is a family member, loved one, a friend or an acquaintance bugging you with the Word of God? Do not turn deaf ears to it, retire into a solitary place and, while alone, carry out an exercise of soul-searching. Do not be shy to acknowledge your sinful nature and then purge yourself of all unrighteousness; by confessing with your mouth that Jesus Christ is Lord and believing in your heart that God raised Him from the death, so you are saved.

It is nothing to be ashamed of. We have all been there, done it and relinquished it to the glory of God through Jesus Christ. I sincerely pray that the contents of this book will ignite in you the kind of fire I experienced in Boston and cause you to take that bold first step to repentance and begin to walk the walk of righteousness.

Shall we say a prayer at this minute for the conversion of our souls? Our heavenly Father I pray you cleanse me with hyssop, and I will be clean; wash me, and I will be whiter than snow. Hide your face from my sins and blot out all my iniquity. Lord, create in me a pure heart, renew a steadfast spirit within me and grant me a willing spirit to sustain me that I may be converted to You. Amen!

TWO

COMING OFF YOUR HIGH HORSES

"Have you noticed how Ahab has humbled himself before me? Because he has humbled himself, I will not bring this disaster in his day. . ." 1Kings 21:29

*B*y humility and the fear of the Lord are riches and honour and life. To enjoy God's uncommon favours, riches, honour and divine blessings, we need to cultivate a childlike faith, and remove any barriers so as to have a close walk with God. The word of God says that unless we change and become like children we will never enter into the kingdom of heaven. So that whoever humbles himself like a child is the greatest in the kingdom of heaven (Matt 18:1-4).

Difficult as it may sound, we are required to identify with children – weak and dependent beings with no status or influence. It is not to be misconstrued what the word of God is saying; we are not to be childish but rather childlike with humble sincere hearts. Children, as we know, are trusting by nature. Children in any given situation, trust adults to look out and do the best for them and, through that trust, their capacity to trust God grows. Therefore the question to pose ourselves when talking the talk, is whether we are behaving childishly in our ways rather than being childlike?

Most times we become so engrossed and preoccupied with our daily routines - be it studies, work, family issues, business, hobbies, and pastimes, you name it, that we lose sight of what really matters, which is the divine purposes of the kingdom of God. It is easy to lose our perspective and chase after temporary short-lived pleasures of life if we let ourselves be carried away with worldly affairs.

Trials and tribulations, more often than not, sway us into a not intended direction of course, derailing us from our walk with God. We are not expected to embrace such distractions, because believe you me, that is all they are. Rather, we are to approach the throne of God in deep humility to receive His instructions, by humbling ourselves, to hear His words.

We are further reassured in His Word, to be precise, in the twenty-fifth psalm that "He guides the humble in what is right and teaches them His way." And as we know, or ought to know, "all the ways of the LORD are loving and faithful toward those who keep the demands of His covenant.

Evidently, it goes without saying that, haughty hearts therefore have no part to play in the kingdom of God. We are not to think of ourselves more highly than we ought, but rather think of ourselves with sober judgment; in accordance with the measure of faith God has for us – according to Romans 12:3. The key therefore to an honest and accurate evaluation, is to know our identity in Christ and what we are worth. I can confidently tell you, we are worth more than many sparrows and, if that is not enough, then I can assure you that, because God loves you and I so much, and places such high value on us that, He gave His only begotten Son that whoever believes in Him should not perish but have everlasting life – John 3:16. A great promise of a death-free life, which is a life without sickness, enemies, evil or sin. A life I will describe as God's life embodied in Christ, given to all who are willing to stop talking the talk and come off their high horses, to confess with their mouths that Jesus Christ is Lord and believe in their hearts that God raised Him from the death, so they are saved. With this assurance, we need not fear difficult trials or personal threats for these cannot dislodge His Holy Spirit from within us.

You will now appreciate that the benefits of humbling oneself and making God the centre of one's life are great. As humble people, we need not yield to ungodly pressures of things done by others or society. This, by far, will not make us non-conformist, arrogant or proud but rather on any given day, obedient children of the most high God.

Take for example the story of Ahab – king of Israel in 1 Kings 16:30 where we are told that he did more evil in the eyes of the Lord, than any of the other kings in Israel, before him. Ahab sold himself to do evil and provoked the anger of God by causing Israel to sin in the sight of God. So that the word of the Lord came to Elijah who went down to meet Ahab and, when he found him, Elijah told him the word of the Lord of the disaster to befall him. To mention but a few, the Lord was going to consume his descendants and cut off from Ahab every last male of Israel – slave or free.

When Ahab heard these words, we are told that, he tore his clothes, put on sackcloth and fasted. He lay in sackcloth and went around meekly. Now sackcloth translated means a garment made of coarse cloth such as sacking, worn formally to indicate mourning, to publicly display extreme grief. Now when he repented in deep humility, God took notice and reduced his punishment *"Have you noticed how Ahab has humbled himself before me? Because he has humbled himself, I will not bring this disaster in his day. . ."* 1Kings 21:29

When our lives fall apart and we turn to God for direction and help, we will hear His word only if we deeply humble ourselves. By the same token, no matter how evil we have been, it is never too late to humble ourselves. The same God who was merciful to Ahab, is inviting you to His kingdom because He wants to be merciful to you, too. Why not turn to Him and ask for forgiveness and He, being faithful and just, will forgive you of your sins and purify you from all unrighteousness. You may wonder, *is this applicable to me*? And *is it really necessary to humble myself*?

IS THIS APPLICABLE TO *ME*?

Yes! The promise of eternal life is not for a selected few but to all mankind, which includes the likes of *you* and *me.* Therefore, to come to the throne of glory, we cannot approach it with a haughty spirit, pride or self-centeredness. This is why we, you and I, are all instructed in Matthew 11 by Jesus Christ, to take His yoke upon us and learn from Him, for He is gentle and humble of heart.

What is this yoke that we are required to take upon us? A yoke is a heavy wooden frame, usually consisting of a bar with an oxbow at either end, for attaching to the necks of a pair of draught animals, especially oxen, so that they can be worked as a team. In this context, the yoke is the heavy burden of sin in our lives. No one person is exempt from it, because the word of God says in Romans 3:23 that we have all sinned and fallen short of the glory of God. It doesn't matter the size and magnitude of our sins, for all sins, whether petty or grave, make us sinners and cut us off from the love of the most high God. Thus if we say that this whole issue of *humility* does not apply to us for whatever reason we may have for talking that talk, then we make God a liar!

But I know and can confidently assure you that God is not a man that He should lie, neither is He the son of man that He should repent. It is pleasing to know that all our sins can be forgiven, because the continuation of the Word of God in the above passage in verse 24, assures us that we are being justified freely by His grace through the redemption that is in Jesus Christ our Lord and Saviour. This is why we are instructed to take the yoke upon us, which is the law of God that guides and points out our sins; and learn from Him with humility, so we can repent and return to God and walk the walk with Him.

IS IT REALLY NECESSARY TO HUMBLE MYSELF?

Without a doubt, I say very much so. The reason being that the essence of humbling yourself before the Lord, is so He will lift you up (James 4:10). As we read earlier, we can only be guided by God in what is right, and taught His way when we walk with Him in humility, which is to say, with a humble spirit worthy of a professed child of God.

The necessity, or better still, the benefit of humbling ourselves is accurately affirmed in the continuation of the verse in Matthew 11 above, when He says "you will find rest for your souls." We will indeed enjoy this promised rest, if we recognise first and foremost, that our worth comes from only God and not man, who is mere mortal. We need not struggle with our own effort but be driven with God's guidance and power, to put Him at the very centre of our lives. We are to submit ourselves totally under His Lordship and relish His undeserved favour. To this end, you should never be found wanting. Your attitude must reflect the humility and self-sac-rifice of Jesus Christ.

Everyone walking the walk, and this by all means, includes those learning or about to, is required to live just as Christ Himself lived. This will be explained fully in a moment, but for now let us look at Uzziah's experience in 2 Chronicles 26.

We are told Uzziah was a remarkably successful king in both war and peace. As a result, his achievements gained him fame and power. He was obedient and sought God's guidance during most of his reign. As long as he sought the Lord, God gave him success and he was greatly helped until he became powerful. However, after Uzziah became powerful, his pride led to his downfall. He was unfaithful to God and challenged God's holiness and took on the role reserved for appointed priests, by trespassing the temple. He even refused to listen to godly counsel to his detriment, thereby bypassing what could have been his opportunity to repent. We are told that he was struck with leprosy and had the detestable and dev-astating disease until the day he died. His pride, of course, went before his destruction and his haughty spirit before his fall (Prov. 16:18). In contrast to Ahab's repentant attitude -

worth emulating - we read that when Ahab repented in deep humility, God took notice and reduced his punishment.

Turning to Christ, gentle and humble of heart, His life on earth began as humbly as could be. He was born in a stable in Bethlehem. When He grew up, He humbled Himself to the will of His Father and taught us, in the Lord's Prayer, how to humble ourselves before God by submitting to His will in our lives, when we pray *"thy will be done."*

Christ was humble and willing to give up His rights to obey God and serve us, making Him a servant king of all ages. Likewise, we should also develop a servant attitude and, be serviceable to serve out of unconditional love for God and all mankind.

In Philippians 2:8 we read *". . . he humbled himself and became obedient to death, even death on a cross."* Death on the cross in the Roman Empire times was a torturous and humiliating public execution of criminals. This was done by nailing their hands and feet to large wooden crosses with vertical and horizontal beams that, crossed one another in a "t" shape. Jesus Christ was by no means a criminal but for your and my sake; He died an agonisingly painful death on that large cross, a symbol of suffering and shame reserved only for criminals. He took up the cross as a servant and died not for Himself, *but* for you and me. Hence, if we are to walk the walk with Him, it is imperative we deny ourselves of worldly pleasures – that are of temporary satisfaction - and take up the cross and follow our humble pace setter - Jesus Christ. Oh what a humble Saviour we have. Are you ready to walk the walk with Him? Or are you still comfortably poised on your high horse?

Recounting the line of conversation I had with my late brother many years ago before his demise, I still can vividly remember and visualise, the expression on his face during that conversation. Though he was older than me, I constantly and boldly engaged him at any given opportune time on talks of the Walk. This is because, judging from our upbringing, I knew he knew how to become humble but he just did not want to do it and, time after time, he refused to take responsibility for his sin. I found it hard to come to terms with his nonchalant actions. Most times he acted like he was not accountable to God and freely talked the talk. Then I thought it was about time I made him stop talking the talk and properly walk the walk; so I took him through a soul-searching exercise. And what would my brother come up with? The usual talk of stop bugging me, I have neither murdered anyone, nor have I stolen another person's property, surely my (careless) love for girls and cigarettes are not a big deal. I patiently heard him out and quietly asked him to turn to the book of James in the bible and respectfully asked him to read James 2:10. He obliged with a smirk and read it while smiling sheepishly but, by the time he had finished reading, that smirk was replaced with some seriousness and he suddenly dropped the holy book in his hand. He asked "Why are you doing this to me?" and I gladly said, this is not my doing, but the will of God for you. Suffice to say, from thereon I began to notice changes in his walk with less talk.

What was the message in James 2:10 that so touched my late brother's being to the point of melting his heart? It was simply this: *"For whoever keeps the whole law and yet stumbles at just one point is guilty of breaking all of it."*

My late brother could have said, why should I even bother, because I cannot keep God's every command, but thankfully he did not use it to justify his sins. He asked for forgiveness where he needed it and renewed his effort to walk the walk as he ought to. These days, we tend not to do what is right because we presume it not to matter. Let us not forget that our exaltation is found in Christ alone. We might begin, like my late brother did, to control our tongues and ask our merciful God for forgiveness where we need it most and either begin walking the walk or continue in the walk.

How does this bring tranquil happiness?

By obeying God, which begins with humility. Obedience to God is fully dealt with in the next chapter. However, the Psalmist in Ps. 131 - in nine very short lines - shows us how, with the following words;

> My heart is not proud, O Lord,
> my eyes are not haughty:
> I do not concern myself with great matters
> or things too wonderful for me
> But I have stilled and quieted my soul;
> like a weaned child with its mother,
> like a weaned child is my soul within me.
> O Israel, put your hope in the Lord
> both now and forevermore.

Trusting and obeying God, as we shall see in the following chapters, positively affects our perspective and gives us the strength and freedom to freely walk the walk. Trust me; you will be walking the walk in honesty because without honesty, a true walk with God is simply impossible. Such tranquil happiness gives us security so that we no longer have to prove ourselves to others, thereby talking the talk with them to self-deception. Our prayer at this juncture is that God forbid that we put ourselves in unfavourable light. Rather, with a humble spirit, to wholly and totally depend on Him.

Are you ready to trust and obey God? Find out how in the next chapter.

THREE

OBEYING AND TRULY SERVING THE LORD

"But be very careful to keep the commandment and the law that Moses the servant of the Lord gave you: to love the Lord your God, to walk in all his ways, to obey his commands, to hold fast to him and to serve him with all your heart and all your soul"- Jos. 22:5

*T*o obey is better than sacrifice! Ever heard of this saying? Very well spoken by Samuel in the Bible, a man who filled many different roles – from judge, priest, counsellor, prophet to God's man – in the book of 1 Samuel 15:22. So also was it echoed in my household over and over again when I was growing up. The reason for this was that my parents were sick and tired of us, the children, trying to pacify them every time we erred by disobeying their instructions. So then, just as Saul disobeyed God's command to go and completely destroy the wicked people, so did we disobey our earthly father's instructions. Though as loving parents they ceaselessly forgave us. It was as much as to say that the sum and substance of proper upbringing consisted in obedience, with which it should always begin, and that atonement was, so to speak, simple appendices.

Looking at this biblically, we see that obedience flows from a heart that is submitted to God's will, a life that is totally surrendered to do His will and that of His alone.

It is not, however, intended to water down sacrifice or render it unimportant, but rather a call to look at the reason for making it. We cannot walk and truly serve God if our hearts are not right with Him. No matter our good deeds and outward actions such as church attendance, prayer, love and offering, to mention but a few, if our hearts are not truly repentant, our sacrifices, then become hollow *unless* they are made with an attitude of love and obedience. We therefore have to be mindful of our heart's attitude towards God to properly walk in obedience to His word.

Abundance of blessings awaits us if only we would learn to trust God and obey Him by taking bold steps of obedience in our walk with Him.

Obedience is defined as the act of submitting to another's will. The biblical definition is clearly explained in Romans 1:5, which reads: *"through Him and for His name's sake, we received grace and apostleship to call people from among all the Gentiles to the obedience that comes from faith."* We are called in our walk with Him, to witness His goodness to all nations and to be an example, of the changed life that Christ has begun in us through the forgiveness of our sins. We cannot, therefore, profess to believe in God or have faith in Him, without submitting ourselves to His will. This is because faith alone is incomplete without obedience. Just as the body without the spirit is dead, so also is faith without deeds - dead. We sincerely need to take heed of this so we are not found wanting.

Likewise, it is not enough to merely talk about believing in what is right without backing our beliefs with action, in other words, doing what faith requires of obedience. No doubt, you would recollect that in chapter one, we mentioned briefly the promises God made with Noah and Abraham in the book of Genesis (6, 12 & 15). Let us together, look at the aspect of their obedience in following God's specific instructions, taking each one of them in turn.

Noah's obedience:

We read earlier that in Genesis 6, God saw how the earth was no longer the perfect paradise He purposed it to be and decided to wipe mankind from the face of the earth, because all humanity forgot Him. There was but one man and his family that still walked the walk with our heavenly Father. His name was Noah. Noah feared and wholeheartedly loved and obeyed God. Noah walked the walk in faith as a living example to his generation. And were there any benefits by way of rewards? Very much so! Noah found favour in God's eyes, in spite of, the multitude of sins he was surrounded by.

So God said to Noah, "I am going to put an end to all people, for the earth is filled with violence because of them. I am surely going to destroy both them and the earth. So make yourself an ark of cypress wood; make rooms in it and coat it with pitch inside and out. This is how you are to build it: The ark is to be 450 feet long, 75 feet wide and 45 feet high. Make a roof for it and finish the ark to within 18 inches of the top. Put a door in the side of the ark and make lower, middle and upper decks. I am going to bring floodwaters on the earth to destroy all life under the heavens, every creature that has the breath of life in it. Everything on earth will perish. But I will establish my covenant with you, and you will enter the ark--you and your sons and your wife and your sons' wives with you. You are to bring into the ark two of all living creatures, male and female, to keep them alive with you. Two of every kind of bird, of every kind of animal and of every kind of creature that moves along the ground, will come to you, to be kept alive. You are to take every kind of food that is to be eaten and store it away as food for you and for them."

Here we are! Noah was specifically instructed to build an ark of cypress wood for him and his family in preparation for the destructive flood that was to come and destroy every living thing on earth. These instructions to the human mind do not make any sense. I would not be surprised if members of his family and indeed everybody he outlined God's specific instructions to, did not believe him. Needless to say, the most important thing is, Noah **believed** and **obeyed** God by quickly getting to work to build the ark to precision. Noah's submission to the will of God is the reason you and me are here today. Destinies may have been altered, had he not obeyed. We too, can find favour in God, if we walk as we ought to, with Him. Just as He promised to keep Noah safe and he believed and trusted God to do as He had promised, let's also trust God for deliverance in the judgment that is sure to come.

Abraham's obedience:

Sin was rampant in the early days notwithstanding God's swift judgment of it; the majority of people continued sinning and ignored God. One of the few, who made an effort to faithfully walk the walk with Him, was Abraham. Like Noah, Abraham found favour in the eyes of God in the godless, self-centred city of Ur and he was promised a God-centred moral nation - Canaan. This was to come about by adhering to specific instructions from God in Gen 12:1-3: ". . .Leave your country, your people and your father's household and go to the land I will show you.

"I will make you into a great nation
and I will bless you;
I will make your name great
and you will be a blessing
I will bless those who bless you

and whoever curses you I will curse

and all peoples on it

will be blessed through you."

So Abraham left as the Lord had told him. He did not doubt his maker's instructions, painful as they may be. Take a moment out and ponder on these instructions. Not an easy task to uproot oneself from a comfort zone so to speak. A bold move would you agree that entails, tearing one-self away from loved family and friends to travel to a completely new country with unfamiliar surroundings. Again, as did Noah, Abraham moved out in **faith** and did as he was told.

He obeyed, left his home and walked the walk with God in the hope of greater blessings in the future. If you are wondering whether or not there were any benefits for Abraham's act of faith, by way of rewards? Trust me, - there were. In fact, it couldn't have been any greater. Why? Because, Jesus Christ, who was born to save humanity, is of Abraham's descent. So that today, through Christ, we can all have a unique personal relationship with God and be blessed beyond measure; only if we confess with our mouth that Jesus Christ is Lord and believe in our heart that God raised Him from the dead, so we are saved. We too can base our right relationship in our walk with God on such unshake-able faith as displayed by Noah and Abraham: heartfelt inner confidence that God is who He says He is and does what He says He will do. Glory to God!

On the other hand, the consequence of disobedience in the walk, if you should ask me, is regrettably destruction. This can surely and truly be avoided, as you will come to learn from Moses' story below.

Moses' disobedience

Now, we learn the Israelites in those days were described as stiff-necked people, who obeyed God for as long as the going was good, and were quick to disobey as soon as, they were faced with difficulties. They never ceased to complain against Moses, who led them with the power of God from Egypt. They even blamed him for bringing them out of Egypt, where they perceived they had plenty to eat and drink. Their journey through the wilderness was no joy to them and they always craved for food and water to drink. As a result, Moses and his brother Aaron went from the assembly of the Israelites, to seek God's face, and God gave Moses specific instructions as we read in Numbers 20:7-12.

"Take the staff, and you and your brother Aaron gather the assembly together. <u>Speak</u> to that rock before their eyes and it will pour out its water. You will bring water out of the rock for the community so they and their livestock can drink."

Though Moses took the staff from the Lord's presence just as he had been commanded, and gathered the assembly together in front of the rock, in his anger he said to them "Listen, you rebels, must we bring you water out of this rock?" He then proceeded to **striking** the rock not once but twice, instead of, *speaking* to it, as he was specifically commanded by God. So then, Moses disobeyed God's specific instructions and dishonoured God by indirectly taking glory for the provision of the drinking water, when in fact, it was God's miracle.

Prior to the birth of Jesus Christ, Moses is described as a man of exemplary character, who it was said was a very humble man, more humble than anyone else on the face of the earth. Moses talked with God and performed awesome miracles at God's command, yet fell short on this occasion when he *struck* the rock rather than *speaking* to it. The truth of the matter is, he was not held to be above reproach and was punished for his disobedience. His punishment was, though he would see the Promised Land from a faraway distance, he would not be the one to bring the Israelites to it. Very sad, harsh or unfortunate one might conclude, but this is the price we pay for the act of disobedience in our walk with God.

As always with our God, there is good news! And in this instance the good news is that, this price can be avoided. As I mentioned earlier, if only we will trust fully in God, and to honour Him as holy in the sight of all, by obeying His commands and/or instructions. It thus goes without saying, that to fully enjoy the benefits of obedience, we are to walk the walk, blameless before our God, revering His authority and appreciating the fact that it is only He that has the power to meet all our needs without exceptions.

Just in case you are thinking this might be too difficult to do, I share those thoughts with you, but remember the law we are to obey and walk in, is a shadow of Christ. Christ has already provided our salvation through His birth and resurrection. The most difficult part of obeying, is simply deciding to start or continue walking with Him now. It is said in Deuteronomy "what I am commanding you today is not too difficult for you beyond your reach." We have the free will to either choose to walk the walk with Him that leads to eternal life, or simply sit back and continue talking the talk, the harvest of which, is condemnation, by which death is inevitable. Are you ready to walk the walk in obedience?

I quite recollect the first time this question was posed to me. It was roughly, about twenty five years ago, after church service one Sunday in the cold bleak mid-winter, still a new-born baby Christian or should I say, toddler, learning to crawl in His ways, still being fed milk alongside occasional solid food, but with some serious teething problems. I looked at my "discipler" - who was assigned to me to mentor me - and thought quietly to myself, this lady is judging my attitude because she did not think I was up to speed, as I ought to. Needless to say, I answered in the affirmative and asked her for help and did not regret it to date.

ARE YOU READY TO WALK IN OBEDIENCE?

Do not hastily give your answer. Ponder carefully on the essence and benefits of so doing, by firstly, concentrating on and digesting the lyrics of John H. Sammis (1887) song Trust and Obey:

1. When we walk with the Lord in the light of His Word,
   What a glory He sheds on our way!

While we do His good will, He abides with us still,

And with all who will trust and obey.

o Refrain:

Trust and obey, for there's no other way To be happy in

Jesus, but to trust and obey.

2. Not a shadow can rise, not a cloud in the skies,

But His smile quickly drives it away;

Not a doubt or a fear, not a sigh or a tear,

Can abide while we trust and obey.

3. Not a burden we bear, not a sorrow we share,

But our toil He doth richly repay;

Not a grief or a loss, not a frown or a cross,

But is blessed if we trust and obey.

4. But we never can prove the delights of His love

Until all on the altar we lay;

For the favour He shows, for the joy He bestows,

Are for them who will trust and obey.

5. Then in fellowship sweet we will sit at His feet,
   Or we'll walk by His side in the way;
   What He says we will do, where He sends we will go;
   Never fear, only trust and obey.

I was guided in this manner:

Give up everything – family, friendship and freedom - in order to know Christ and His resurrection power, which is the evidence of our destiny. If Abraham did, when he was instructed to leave his country, his people and his father's household and go to the land that God was to show him, then so too can you and I. Unlike us, Noah and Abraham did not have the Holy Bible, which I call God's manual for righteous living, to guide them. Nevertheless, they believed, obeyed and launched out in faith and did as they were told by God. We have access to this knowledge and this power, but to tap into it fully, we have to make some serious sacrifices, in order to enjoy its full benefits.

Today, what are you willing to give up in order, to know Christ and walk in His ways with Him? The acts of the sinful nature, which we must give up, we are informed, are obvious: sexual immorality, impurity and debauchery (now debauchery means excessive sensual indulgence such

as smoking, drinking, overeating, lies, addictives etc); idol-
atry and witchcraft; hatred, discord, jealousy, fits of rage,
selfish ambition, dissensions, factions and envy; drunken-
ness, orgies, and the like. We are warned that those who
live like this, will not inherit the kingdom of God (Galatians
5:19-21).

Whatever it is, that you need to give up today to enable
you to make the right choice to walk the walk, right this
minute, I want you to know that knowing Christ is more
than worth the sacrifice. It is also worth pointing out that
no amount of law keeping, self-improvement, discipline or
religious effort, can make us right with God. This is because
righteousness comes from God. We are or can only be made
righteous, by trusting in Jesus Christ and being born again.

Being born again is simply to be reborn spiritually and to
receive new life from God. Through that faith in Christ, this
new birth changes us from inside out. It rearranges firstly, our
attitudes, that is, the way we view things or tend to behave
towards it, usually in an evaluating manner. Secondly, our
desires, which are our expressed wishes or requests or cravings, to include sexual appetite. Thirdly, our *motives* in life.
In other words, our reason for taking the particular course
of action. Being born again, thus makes us spiritually alive,

which means we can draw near to God, hold unswervingly in faith, encouraging one another and fellowshipping together in the faith we profess. And it gives us personal access to God twenty-four/seven.

Attitudes - Does your attitude reflect values of the world or of Christ? Christ's basic principles and values should be the foundation of our thinking and actions. That is, if we are to sincerely walk the walk with Him in the knowledge of His word and commit ourselves to Him one hundred percent. The walk values are contained in Matt. 5:3-12. One of my pastors put it in a logical way, which made so much sense to me when he said in Church one Sunday morning that, the beatitudes were not written to increase our knowledge, but to make us live better lives. It was not a manifesto – God's public declaration of intent, policy or aims, but a constitution – the fundamental principles by which to live our lives. In other words, with the right attitude, we can reap the full blessings, joy, hope and benefits of our walk with God.

For those who are poor in spirit, theirs is the kingdom of heaven, those who mourn will be comforted, and the meek will inherit the earth. As for those who hunger and thirst for righteousness, they will be filled. The merciful will be shown mercy; the pure in heart will see God, while the peacemakers will be called sons of God. As for those who are persecuted because of righteousness, theirs is the kingdom of heaven.

It has been said that, sin began with our wrong attitude to various aspects of life, causing us to set unbiblical standards, for others to follow. However, in the New Testament scriptures, Jesus Christ pointed out that sin, actually begins in the attitudes and intentions of the inner person. We are not pure because of our outward acts, we become pure on the inside as Christ renews our minds and transform us into His image.

Desires - Are your desires geared towards how to do what God wants you to do? In 1 Chr. 29:19, David, before he died, asked God to give his son, Solomon, wholehearted devotion to keep God's commandments. This means entire dedication to God. Do you find it hard to do what God wants you to do or even harder to want to do it? God can give you a wholehearted devotion today, if you believe in Jesus Christ and take the bold step to walk the walk with Him, to god's glory. This is in fact already happening in you, as you toy with the decision, because God works within us to will and to act according to His good purpose. Therefore if you love the Lord, hate evil, and I pray you do, so He will guard your life and deliver you from the hand of the wicked.

We cannot walk with God without first and foremost, searching our hearts, to see that our desires are not drawn to, what is evil but to pleasure and fulfilment according to His rules and definitely, not our selfish rules. We must, therefore, not take part in wicked deeds with men who are evildoers. Falling in line requires us to, ask God *today* because tomorrow might be *too* late, to change us on the inside.

Motives in life - whatever you determine in your heart to do, check your conscience to see that it is not a foolish idea, which will turn into foolish actions. For if we fail to eliminate our wrong thoughts and motives, it will cause us grief, just as it caused Aaron and Miriam, when they opposed Moses *(Num. 12)*.

A stumbling block in life, that we fail to realise, is that our selfish motives are a barrier to prayer. We must therefore, be filled with the power of the Holy Spirit, to accomplish God's new purpose in our lives and embrace the fruit of the spirit. The fruits of the Holy Spirit are the spontaneous work of the Holy Spirit in us, which produces the character traits that are found in Jesus Christ. This is what I refer to, as walking the walk with the right attitude, desires and motives in obedience to the Word of God.

We cannot walk in partial obedience to God, by allowing the foolishness of this world, to sway us into the wrong direction. We need to take a stand and let our walk tell our story. A friend's husband once visited my office to consult with my legal services. While in conference with the gentleman, our discussion took a different dimension altogether, and I found, we had digressed from considering the prospects of his case, to sharing our experiences in the walk. He narrated his initial setbacks, which made so much sense to me. He had tried to please both God and man - in this case, his old friends of the world and had in fact, believed he was in control of, and could single-handedly, handle the situation. He was of the opinion that he could compromise his obedience to God's command and even negotiate it. Wrong! You need to take a stand. Lukewarm-ness is a halfway house and it's repugnant in the Kingdom of God to say the least. Well, let us continue with my client's narration. As a result, he still kept his association with his old friends and went out with them to night clubs. He socialised with them as he used to do, that is to say; prior to giving his life to Christ to walk with Him. Whilst out there with them, he was very happy, so he thought, but soon realised that such happiness was short-lived. Whenever he got back home and laid on his bed, he had not an iota of inner peace, as compared to, the times when he returned home from fellowshipping, that is, meeting with other Christians.

He soon realised that it was pointless yielding to peer pressure, by walking with those friends, without substance to challenge his destiny or future for that matter. Whenever he returned from an outing with them and hung his jacket, unlike his fellowship meeting, the same reeked of cigarette and polluted the air around him. It became apparent to him that he had to make a choice between life and death. Of course, he chose life, to continue in his walk with God. We too can today obey God's instructions, without reservations and doubts, to seek first, His Kingdom and His righteousness, so as to, receive Jesus Christ as our Saviour.

Or, on the contrary, we can disobey and reject Jesus Christ, and be in darkness forever without Him. The choice is clear. Receive God's gift of Life - His Son Jesus Christ!

Choose life and walk the walk to God's glory through Jesus Christ.

Obeying and truly serving God in sincerity, will keep us all from harm, catastrophes and diseases or sickness. God has promised that if we listen, carefully to His voice and do what is right in His eyes, and if we pay attention to His commands and keep all His decrees, He will not allow upon us, the diseases unleashed on the Egyptians, but rather, as our faithful God, He will heal us.

We can begin to do this, by resolving to make the main purpose of our life's work, service to God and man. This requires us, to love God more than anything under the sun, with all our hearts, with all our souls and with our entire minds. We are to be selfless and love our neighbours, as ourselves. Why do not you explore with me in the next chapter the selfless nature of the walk?

FOUR

SELFLESS LIFESTYLE

"May God himself, the God of peace, sanctify you through and through. May your whole spirit, soul and body be kept blameless at the coming of our Lord Jesus Christ. The one who calls you is faithful and he will do it" (1Thess. 5:23).

*E*xperience divine joy, to the maximum in this walk of righteousness, by truly practising and actualising the letters, in the spelling of joy, in such chronological manner, that is - putting **J**esus Christ first, **O**thers second and **Y**ourself third.

Our daily lifestyle must mirror this, thereby disregarding ourselves or our own interests, to take up the command and challenge, to trust in our God wholeheartedly with our souls, bodies and minds and to love our neighbours as ourselves. What a joy to walk with the Lord! Amazing, I will say, and I'm loving every second and every bit of it.

Putting Jesus Christ first in all that we do requires us, to respect and recognise who He is. We can achieve this with divine wisdom, if we ask, and surely, if our aim for asking, is not self-centred but God-centred. There is no doubt in my mind that vividly striking positive changes in our lifestyle, are made to the glory of God. In my daily walk with God, I have constantly experienced the divine joy and uncommon favours of God, by burying haughtiness of heart, and embracing humility in my obedience, to His commands.

He has said in one of my favourite passages in the bible - and I know that the majority of those who know me very well, will agree that I have shared it with them, and have in fact challenged them to its application, in their daily lifestyles: Our God commanded and promised us, in Ex. 23: 24-26 that as long as we "do not bow down to other gods or worship them or follow their practices . . . and worship the Lord God, He will bless our food and water. He will take away sickness from among us and none will miscarry or be barren in our land. He will give us a full life span." And in Exodus 14:13-14, we are reassured and commanded ". . .not to be afraid. But to stand firm and we will see the deliverance the LORD will bring us today. The Egyptians you see today you will never see again. The LORD will fight for you; you need only to be still."

It is accepted we live in a world whose norms and values, are inconsistent with the values of the walk, but this call from God, is one of faith-maintaining lifestyle - an epitome of right living, in the sight of God who is faithful, to do what He has promised to do. In effect, rather than being hostile and despairing in the walk of eternal life with God, we need to be encouraged by God's word and promises; and STAND FIRM and watch the excellent way God would deliver us from all ills.

Perhaps a brief explanation of what is meant by "other gods" in the passage above is worth our discussion. Other gods are images of a god, idol or person, who is greatly adored or admired. In short, anything under the sun we submit to, taking pre-eminent position in our lives, to the extent that we yield, to its authority or control, is a god to us.

Having so explained, and with the meaning grasped, I cannot adequately emphasise that, in our selfless walk with God, we must, as a matter of reverence to our supreme omniscient God, put obeying God first, above all else, and before conforming to the norms and values of our society.

We need to be mindful of that fact that our God, is a jealous God and He will not give His glory to another or His praise to idols. He has specifically commanded - you shall have no other gods before Him and we are to worship and serve Him only.

Is it really worth serving idols?

With or without my experience in the walk, my response to this would not have been anything short of an emphatic NO!

As a matter of fact, the so-called unconventional and unorthodox demands of these gods that lead to nothing, but misery and disarray in families, and to all involved and concerned, makes it a definite no-go venture, for all children of God walking the walk with Him.

Moving on, would you agree with me that; amidst difficult times, trials and tribulations, the lowest of low pitfalls, we need to be assured that we have a supernatural helper, at our beck and call, ready and able to come to our aid and **protect** us, and not vice versa? I definitely and very certainly, like you, too, would not want a god that would have to be carried, with our own hands to safety in the face of calamity. Surely not!

A very good reason why *Elijah* in the book of 1 Kings:18 taunted and mocked the idolaters to shout louder because their god may be either in deep thought, busy, travelling or sleeping and must be awakened. That is a burlesque!

Oh, what a great joy to know that our God, with whom we walk, is One who watches over our lives; He will neither slumber nor sleep, better put in Ps. 121:

I lift up my eyes to the hills
where does my help come from?
My help comes from the Lord
the maker of heaven and earth

He will not let my foot slip
he who watches over me will not slumber
indeed, he who watches over Israel
will neither slumber nor sleep

The Lord watches over me
the Lord is your shade at your right hand

the sun will not harm me by day

nor the moon by night

The Lord will keep me from all harm

he will watch over my life

the Lord will watch over my coming and going

both now and forevermore. *(Amen)*

It is definitely about time and, if I may say so, long overdue, to stop talking the talk, and let God's word speak personally to us. We cannot profess our faith and be confident in our walk, if we lack substance that comes with the knowledge of the Word. Today, we have the privilege, to easy access of the circulation of God's laws as outlined in the bible. This is to be with us, to read all the days of our lives, that we may learn to revere the Lord our God. We are to follow carefully, all the words of the law and decrees, and to, *not* consider ourselves better than others, or turn from it to the right or to the left. In that knowledge, we will need to get rid of anything that will stand between our walk, or be a hindrance or reproach, to our conscious effort, to sincerely walk the walk. Consequently, by such commendable determination, our morals and association with others will inevitably be enhanced; likewise our crowned glory on completion of the walk.

Let us look at the story of *Achan's* sin in Joshua 7, by way of shedding more light on the above.

Prior to *Achan's* sin, the Israelites had won various battles, the latest being their victory in Jericho. God helped them so that they conquered all their enemies. Going to the next city, Ai, was not to be a problem, as Joshua perceived it, because he was confident that with God on his side, their enemies could not triumph over them. Coupled with the fact that the spies he sent to Ai, had come back with favourable reports that there were not many people there. Needless to say, they were defeated, much to their surprise. They became afraid and disheartened. Amidst this disappointment, Joshua tore his clothes, and the elders sprinkled dust over their heads, and approached the throne of God, to find out what was wrong. He needed to find out why God had brought them over the Jordan at all, and to deliver them into the hands of the Amorites, to destroy them.

God asked Joshua to get up, for Achan has caused Israel to sin by violating God's covenant, which He had commanded them. Not only had Achan taken some of the devoted things, but has stolen, lied and put those things with his own possessions, as a result of which Israel could not stand against their enemies. God was irate, and said He would not be with them anymore, unless they destroyed what was devoted to destruction, when they defeated Jericho.

Achan, though he hid his sin from men, could not hide it from the omniscient God, who knew and specifically instructed Joshua, on the steps to take, to expose Achan. Joshua followed God's instructions and Achan, on being named, confessed that he had indeed sinned before God. He had taken some silver coins, a large wedge of pure gold and a beautiful Babylonian garment from Jericho. They were all buried in the ground under his tent. Joshua sent messengers who ran to look and came back with the accursed things. Because of his sin, the Lord indeed troubled Achan for not keeping His word.

As we see from the story of Achan's sin, our quest, insatiable appetite, and cravings for selfish desires, and hidden agendas, not only affect us individually in our walk, but also affect those walking with us. It is thus enough, to reiterate that sin has many consequences, none of which is good. This is beautifully echoed in Prov. 4: 23-27:

Above all else, guard your heart

For it is the wellspring of life

Put away perversity from your mouth

Keep corrupt talk far from your lips

Let your eyes look straight ahead

Fix your gaze directly before you

Make level paths for your feet

And take only ways that are firm

Do not swerve to the right or to the left

Keep your foot from evil

Our selfless walk of righteousness with God requires us, to honour one another above ourselves, putting the needs of other people - be it our earthly parents, siblings, children, friends, acquaintances, strangers and the like - besides Jesus Christ, ahead of our own interests. A display of some sense of sensitivity and empathy is expected, in our dealings with fellow mankind. Remember, God created us all in His own image and we are commanded to be completely humble, gentle, patient, bearing with one another in love, making an effort to keep the unity of the spirit through the bond of peace. In living a selfless lifestyle in our walk, it is prudent for us to be mindful of the fact that no one is perfect, hence the need to respect, regard and protect others, in spite of their weaknesses, shortcomings or faults. If need be, rather than being peeved, by their unpleasant actions, we may admonish one another in love and with all wisdom, because the entire law is summed up in a single command, *"Love your neighbour as yourself."*

Actualisation of this command in our walk, on a daily basis, compels us to adopt and practice sacrificial love. We can obey this command, by being there for one another, helping others with tenderness of heart, encouraging one another in good spirit and in prayers as well.

To effectively do this, we have to cultivate the attitude of, listening to others with listening ears, and giving generously to others without holding back, whenever we are in a position to do so. What a joy of harmonious relationship this will be. What more could be good and pleasant than to walk together in unity with others?

Otherwise, if we keep on biting and devouring each other, we will be destroyed by each other. In the book of James, we are commended for doing right, if we keep the royal law above. We thus have to recognise the rights of others, enemies inclusive; and behave wisely and justly, in order to establish and/or restore a godly relationship with them, to glorify our Maker.

However, if on the other hand, we show favouritism, we sin and are convicted by law, as lawbreakers. This is definitely not consistent with the walk, thus the key word in putting others' before ours is, love. The act of loving, and its dynamics, of knowing God, through a personal relationship with Jesus Christ, will be dealt with later on in this book.

Meanwhile, attaining the crown of glory in our walk, thus entails loving one another genuinely - because it is in loving - not being loved - that the heart is blessed, and it is in giving - not in seeking gifts - that we find our quest to do God's will. Our knowledge of the word of God is a paramount prerequisite, in our walk with Him. We can only grasp it, if we constantly read our Bible and meditate on it day and night, carefully doing everything that is written in it.

Difficult and tasking you might say, or be thinking, but, I can assure you, it is not as challenging as you may think, if we ask God for the spirit of understanding and discernment, when we read it; so as to get the main gist of whatever passage and message is read. I, pray that prayer whenever I pick up my Bible to read, because it is of no use to me, reading and not understanding what I have read. How then can I obey and apply the law in my walk, if I am at a loss of its contents? Little or insignificant as the prayer may sound, it works wonders for me, my little secret, but I guess no longer a secret, because I have gladly shared it with you now. I challenge you; right this moment, to put it to the test in faith.

A question I always ask myself, in this aspect of my walk, when carrying out one of my soul-searching exercises is, how do others perceive me? The word of God tells me in Isaiah 60:1 *"Arise, shine for your light has come, and the glory of God rises upon you."* Is the glory of the Lord really upon me? Am I shining in the light of God? I always say to myself, if I can answer yes to these questions, then I am blessed; if not, it is not too late to receive that blessing.

I am perpetually yearning for this blessing, so I was thrilled some fourteen years ago, when I went into a stationery store, to shop for some office stationery, as I had newly set up my law practice, to practise on my own account. I noticed a couple in the store, and the pattern of our encounter, is one never to be forgotten. The couple in question crossed me in every aisle I stopped to shop. I became rather weary and suspicious of their agenda. I dared not lock eyes with them, which was what I perceived they were waiting to happen. Instead, I resolved within me that come what may, I will not give them that joy - not that day or ever. Lo and behold, unbeknown to me, they had some pleasant words for me. The lady slowly edged her way to me, and from the corner of my eyes, I saw the gentleman drawing closer, until they were literally inches away from me. I had no choice, in the circumstances, other than to look in their direction, to acknowledge their presence. The gentleman was the first to break the ice, by attempting to exchange pleasantries, and the lady jumped in, and said "beautiful lady, my husband and I could not resist the aura around you, the calmness and serenity is captivating, so we have been following you around the store." The gentleman smiled and nodded in agreement, and I thought to myself, these two have no urgent business to transact. I almost leant on my own understanding, to brush aside their compliments, but an inner voice quickly spoke quietly to me, prompting me to show appreciation and give glory to God. I immediately got myself together, with the biggest grin you can ever imagine, stretching from one end of my cheek to the other, and said "It is the glory of God." We parted, knowing that I am walking with a living God, and indeed shining, because His light and glory has risen upon me.

Don't we all long for the fulfilment of His promises in our lives? I don't know about you, but I always enjoy them, because they give me the "feel-good" factor; knowing that our heavenly Father, has woven together our lives into His plan. The assurance of Him, being in control of history, and manifesting in our walk with Him, at a perfect timing, is absolutely awesome.

In a similar fashion, shortly after my above recounted encounter, I attended one of our law annual weekend conferences, held in a little town outside of London. On the morning of the conference, one male delegate seated opposite from me, at a round table we shared, kept looking at me in a rather funny way, so I asked him if there was a problem. I was blown away by his seemingly bold question, wanting to know what I was doing seated at the conference table. I replied with a question – what are you doing here? He proudly replied he was a lawyer attending the law conference, and I burst his bubble with my response - likewise myself. Little did I know that a lady seated next to me, was eavesdropping on our conversation and she turned and offered her comforting words, saying; I must pardon the gentleman because truly, I do not look anything like them – that is, stressed and overbearing, but rather, quite calm and serene. I was ecstatic because, yet again, someone had seen exactly what I saw in the lady, who played a significant part in my Boston Experience. To me, these instances, created an opportunity for me to testify, of the goodness of God and my walk with Him. I shall continue to walk the walk because God wants me to and the same goes for you, too. Evidently stated in Prov. 2:20.

> Thus you will walk in the ways of good men
> and keep to the paths of the righteous.
> For the upright will live in the land
> and blameless will remain in it,
> but the wicked will be cut off from the land
> and the unfaithful will be torn from it.

On the contrary, do others perceive me, as somewhat a hypocrite? I sincerely pray not. Otherwise I would have been walking a worthless walk, which I sincerely, do not intend to. Of course, I will be perceived a hypocrite, if I act like I am walking the walk, and it turns out I am not. I am mindful of the fact that our attitudes towards others mirror our relationship with God, In which case, we cannot really and truly walk the walk, if we have and harbour unresolved issues with our family, friends and colleagues. We are hypocrites and will only be deceiving ourselves in this walk, if all our actions show and portray our love for God, and yet we hate others. How can we then say we love God – whom we have not set eyes on - and are walking with Him, when we cannot love and forgive our friends, family and colleagues that we see day in and day out, created in God's image? We become liars. Remember, our command is - whoever loves God must love his brother (others).

Furthermore, in loving your neighbour as yourself, conscious effort must be made, to ensure that we do not lead them into temptation, that is, to committing sin. Have you ever heard it said, "one man's meat is another man's poison"? While one man's faith allows him to eat everything, another man, whose faith is weak, only eats vegetables. We are all different in nature and taste. It would therefore be wrong of me to compel, push and pressure others into liking what I like. Or to impose my cultural values, or force them to accept my views, which may be distasteful to them, recognizing that they feel they cannot object, being weaker persons.

Likewise, the story of Eve's sin was as a result of her heeding the serpent's deceitful command, to eat the forbidden fruit that God had specifically instructed them not to eat. Eve lured Adam into eating it with her, and clearly flouted the word of God, and caused Adam to sin. Their disobedience, as we all know, affected all mankind, causing a twist in fate. It is worth noting that because our freedom and responsibility in the walk are inseparably tied together, our actions must uncompromisingly be guarded. By so doing, we walk a measured pace to live the life which we speak, not causing others in the walk or about to step out and walk, to stumble and fall.

We have no excuse not to walk in accordance to God's word because, in any given situation, no matter our cultural background, we need not live a lifestyle just because it is praised and acceptable by society. This is not to be construed as rebelling, against the norms and values of a given society; rather we are to wisely adjust our culture, as long as we do not compromise God's laws. Remember, we are warned by way of godly instructions in Romans 12:2, to not conform to the pattern of this world, which are usually selfish and corrupting, but to be transformed, with the help of the Holy Spirit, educating, directing and renewing our mind. Then we will be able, to test and approve what God's will is—His good, pleasing and perfect will to live and honour Him. This way, we give our lives as living sacrifices for His service.

Actions – you would appreciate- speak louder than words. Is your walk therefore, speaking louder than your talk? We cannot profess to be walking with God and behave foolishly. As we all know, foolishness leads to disorder and it goes without saying, that the act of foolishness, fans the fire of discord. Our character generally must embody peace, winsome speech and loving words; in short, our conduct in the walk, must back our talk, if we are still talking very loudly. This is what really does matter, and not our religious activities, short of practically actualising the Word. In 1John 3:18, we are commanded as dear children of God walking the walk with Him, to not love with words or speech, but with actions and in truth. We thus, have to measure the pace of our walk, to see how clearly our gaits - in the form of our actions - say we love our neighbours. How generous are we with our time, money and possessions, to help those in need?

This, I will say, is some very good food for thought, and not in the least, to be ignored. But more importantly, these deeds of loving service, to our neighbours, are not to be substituted for our faith in Jesus Christ, but rather, a verification of such faith in Him.

Hence, whoever is wise and understanding will show it, by a good and selfless lifestyle, by deeds done in humility that flows and comes from wisdom. In which case, if you sincerely love God – and I mean love Him with all your heart – then you will walk in a manner, to let your light so shine before others, that they may see your good deeds and praise your Father in heaven - Glory! The beatitudes, as we read earlier on, were pronounced, not written, and founded on the principle of love your neighbour as you would love yourself. With these values and benefits in mind, are you ready to now sincerely walk the walk in loving-kindness and taste the goodness that comes with it? If so, Read on!

FIVE

EXPRESSLY LIVING LOVE FOR GOD

". . .through whom we have gained access by faith into this
grace in which we now stand. And we rejoice in the hope
of the glory of God. Not only so, but we also rejoice in our
sufferings, because we know that suffering produces per-
severance; perseverance, character; and character, hope.
And hope does not disappoint us, because God has poured
out his love into our hearts by the Holy Spirit, whom He
has given us. . ."- Rom. 5:2-5

*L*ove so amazing, so divine, demands my soul, my
life, my all. Thus I shall fear God and keep His commandments, for this is the whole duty, my all. I call this, the
perfect antidote, for the infirmities of the title of this book.

For those of us walking the walk, to have purpose-driven direction in our walk, we need to fear God and keep His commandments. And to those talking the talk, it is either a wake-up call, or a reminder that on the Day of Judgment, God will analyse and review how His commandments, were responded to. It is never too late in the day, to give our feet to go His way, vowing to take every step carefully, within the parameters of His commandments, no matter what the mysteries and apparent contradictions of this world.

My son is mystified about this notion of "fear of God" and is always asking why is it that he should fear God, if indeed God is the loving Father He is said to be. No amount of explaining seems to help change the underlying fact in his mind, because the question keeps popping up every now and again. This is one aspect of faith; he has yet to come to terms with. I am confident and know, the older he grows and wiser he becomes, the better he will comprehend, with broadened understanding that there is no fear in love, for perfect love drives out fear, so that the one who fears is not made perfect in love.

In essence, walking with Him out of love, the bedrock of our relationship with Him, builds up our confidence in Him, to the extent that, fear, is conquered. This way, the

more focused we are on His love; the easier it is, to overcome fear. The Word of God says that if we love Him, we
will obey what He commands and His teaching, and He will
love us and make His home with us. What then is this love,
you may ask?

Ordinarily, love, the greatest of all human qualities, is
defined as deep affection or fondness for a person or thing.
Little or no meaning is given to love in this modern age,
because of the confusion surrounding what true love is.

The love referred to here, is the brotherly love, usually
referred to, as agape love. We uphold this kind of forgiving
and all-encompassing love in our walk, when we exhibit it
through our genuine love for one another. This kind of love
can only come from our fear of God, by this it is meant, the
reverence for God. And everyone who loves is born of Him,
because God is love and not vice versa. He demonstrated His
love for you and me, when He sent His only begotten Son
into this world that we might live through Him. The sole prerequisite of the walk, is acknowledging Jesus Christ as the
Son of God, by confessing with our mouth that Jesus Christ
is Lord and believing in our hearts that God raised Him from
the death, so we are saved. We say we love God because
He first loved us. Let us thus stop talking the talk and truly

demonstrate, and act our talk through the steps of our walk, of unselfish love for others.

We too can demonstrate our love for God, with our generous giving, in all areas of our life, with family, friends and the Church, which is the body of Christ. We are indeed commanded in Luke 6:38, to give and it will be given to us, a good measure, pressed down, shaken together and running over. For with the measure we use, it will be measured to us.

The best way to discharge this act of sacrificial giving in kindness and generosity - so as to be endowed with the divine qualities of prosperity, compassion and grace - is to give in secret. In other words, when you give, do not let your left hand know what your right hand is doing, so that your giving may be in secret. Be very discreet with your giving and avoid showing and telling of the act. Then God, who sees what is done in secret, will reward you.

By the same token, we are warned not to be deceived, because God cannot be mocked, for with whatever intentions we give, we will reap in full measure. As we profess to be walking with the Creator, let us give as if we are giving directly to Him; this way we honour our Creator and the Creation.

In living love for God, we make our love a reflection of the steadfast love that is freely given to us by God Himself. To remain from everlasting to everlasting, with those who faithfully and sincerely walk the walk with Him - not excluding those who keep His covenant - fear Him and remember to obey Him. The manifestation of this is portrayed through our sacrificial giving and service to others, without expectation of earthly reward in return. We fail in our walk, if all we do is simply talk - as those talking the talk - about how we feel love for others, without practising and actualising the perfect love. The Word of God teaches us in John 15:13 that "Greater love has no one than this that He lay down His life for His friends." You and I can be His friends if we do what He commands, which is . . . *"Love the Lord your God with all your heart and with your soul and with all your mind . . . Love your neighbour as yourself"* (Matt. 22:37).

This brings to mind a personal experience of God's amazing grace. I was in the shower some time ago, when I had cause to answer a distress telephone call, from a very close friend of mine. I was in the bathroom as usual, having my quiet time with God. I must confirm in a noisy household such as mine, with teenagers all striving for special attention, at any given opportunity, and noisily squabbling over petty palaver, the only room in the house with peace and quiet, is the bathroom, where I usually retire to have a one-on-one talk with God. This is therapeutic with a pick-me-up sensational flavour, as an add-on in the walk of righteousness. You too can practice and experience it in your walk, if you have not already done so. Do you really want to learn how to have such conversation with God? Find out how in the ensuing chapters.

Anyway, I answered the call; my dear friend narrated her difficulties about a situation in which she found herself. She had successfully completed her degree course, and was due to attend her graduation ceremony. She had invited some of her pastors from her church, to support her on her big day. She found out she did not have sufficient money to cater for her invited guests, from paying for their tickets for the day, to hosting them to refreshment after the occasion.

Her main reason for calling me was not to request financial assistance, but to pick my brain on the best way to politely de-invite the pastors, whilst saving face in the process. I found myself contemplating what I would have done in a similar situation, and without second thought I advised her not to carry out her plan, and ended our conversation, by offering to foot the entire bill.

Now, while in the shower, it was laid on my heart, to give her a little more than she required. I got personal with God, with my excuses of this friend having a spouse. Surely he could chip in with the additional sum of money, I was being asked to give her, on top of, what I had agreed with her prior to ending our conversation. It was a tough assignment, but needless to say, I obeyed. The interesting bit was the call from my friend, when she received the money in her account. In her excitement, she sang praises to God, for having answered her prayers, telling me that we indeed, serve an active and living God. She proceeded to volunteer information, on how she had prayed to God, to touch my heart, to give her more than what we had concluded, because what she hadn't mentioned to me earlier on was that she had invited a neighbour, too. We both expressed gratitude to God and I jokingly warned her not to pray that kind of prayer anymore, that is, where I'm concerned. After we both hung up our respective phones, I thanked God for considering me, a useful vessel for noble purposes, and using me on that day to put a smile on my friend's face, to His glory.

Painful and pocket-pinching as it may have seemed at the time, the amazing grace of God saw me through. Humility, obedience, love and all that we have read above, came into play to make me walk the walk, faithfully that day. I had to go the extra mile, to sacrificially give to another, a worthwhile course, if you should ask me.

Are you synchronising love, the greatest of all human qualities, with all the other commandments in your walk with Him? If not, we can start now, by obeying His commands.

Firstly, by practising and actualising it from the home front, in our relationships with our family members.

Secondly, at our workplace in the manner in which we discharge our call of duty, whether or not our bosses or supervisors are present and,

Thirdly, how we treat our subordinates - without partiality.

In a nutshell, our relationships, the way we relate to our family and friends, how we use our money, the way we serve our bosses, how we treat our enemies; and all that concerns us, must reflect the reality of the Word in our walk.

This is beautifully encapsulated and stated in Ephesians 6:1-9 as follows:

Children, obey your parents in the Lord, for this is right.
Honour your father and mother--which is the first com-

*mandment with a promise-- that it may go well with you
and that you may enjoy long life on the earth. Fathers, do
not exasperate your children; instead, bring them up in the
training and instruction of the Lord.*

*Slaves, obey your earthly masters with respect and fear,
and with sincerity of heart, just as you would obey Christ.
Obey them not only to win their favour when their eye is
on you, but like slaves of Christ, doing the will of God from
your heart. Serve wholeheartedly, as if you were serving the
Lord, not men, because you know that the Lord will reward
everyone for whatever good he does, whether he is slave
or free. And masters, treat your slaves in the same way. Do
not threaten them, since you know that he who is both their
Master and yours is in heaven, and there is no favouritism
with him.*

Wow! Isn't the word of God so sweet? Sweeter than
honey to the mouth I will aver - as we gain understanding
from His precepts - thereby hating every wrong path, in our
walk. You and I can also live this love for God with ease as
Dorcas did in ages past.

Dorcas' sacrificial love

Now Dorcas, also called Tabitha, expressly lived love for God as we read in Acts 9:36-42. Dorcas was a disciple who made a vast impression in the lives of the people in her community. She was an outstanding character in her community, who touched the hearts of many, with her acts of generosity; she gave freely without expecting anything in return. This would have demanded her time, money and personal involvement. She was well known among her peers as one who went about, always doing good and helping the poor. She selflessly attended to their needs, stitching them robes and other clothing items. Unfortunately, as the saying goes "nothing good lasts forever." Dorcas became ill and died; what a devastating loss to her community. Her body was washed and placed in an upstairs room.

Although the community was mourning the loss of an important part of the family of believers, a most loved one, they had hope she will live again - and so great was their faith - that with God all things are possible. In that instance, they sent for Peter, one of Jesus' disciples and asked him to come at once.

Upon arrival, Peter was taken to the upstairs room where they had placed Dorcas' body. The room was filled with mourners. All the widows and perhaps those she had helped, were crying and showing the robes and other clothing items, that Dorcas had made, while she was alive. Peter, I am certain, may have been moved, by such overwhelming evidential proof. He sent everyone out and knelt down to pray, and turning to Dorcas' corpse said, "Tabitha, get up." She opened her eyes and sat up. The good news of God restoring her back to life spread throughout the region, causing many to believe in the Lord.

Our story too can be told, if we walk the walk with good deeds, appropriate for those who profess to worship and walk with God. We can begin utilising our talents, to the benefit of others, through our service to the Creation, especially, the powerless widows and orphans. By serving and looking after them in their distress and keeping ourselves from being polluted by the world, to God's glory.

AM I DOING THIS AND WALKING RIGHT?

Perhaps it is about time we took stock of our lives – my favourite soul-searching exercise – to determine whether or not we are doing as Dorcas did and more, to justify our faithful walk. If at this stage we are still talking the talk and haven't tamed our tongues, then we seriously have to repent big time. Scripturally, we cannot consider ourselves religious and yet not keep tight reins on our tongues. In other words, we must stop talking the talk and control our speech more effectively. Rather than saying negative things to brag, manipulate, bring others down, gossiping or lying and many other things, we could be looking at what to say to encourage others, lift up their spirits, motivate and inspire them to give glory to God. Our energies could be burned in our acts of generous giving, service to the community, the church and to good and worthy causes. We will be doing what Dorcas did - whether insignificant or not, it was worthy to be recorded in the Word of God - if we pay particular attention to one another's needs and expressly live love, as we are commanded to. Then we too may echo the joy of harmonious relationships, as David did in Psalm 133 when he said,

How good and pleasant it is
when God's people live together in unity!
It is like precious oil poured on the head,
running down on the beard,

running down on Aaron's beard,

down on the collar of his robe.

It is as if the dew of Hermon

were falling on Mount Zion.

For there the Lord bestows his blessing,

even life forevermore.

Mind you, we must abound in the love of God and have a relationship with Him, through the knowledge of Him, to be able to love others. Do you truly love God?

TESTING THE PACE OF WALK

The true pace of our walk is tested by the nature of our paces. By this I mean, the manner of walking or the rate of progression, of any various gaits. Are we still strong and very courageous? We are not to be terrified nor be discouraged, for the Lord our God is with us and will be with us wherever we go. He has commanded us and He is faithful and just to do whatever He commands. By now the joy of our walk, should have brought us enlightenment of the eyes, with purity of life. If not, I urge you to keep walking with Him. Embrace the spirit of patience in your walk and just enjoy the experience, knowing that you are glorifying God with every honourable gait of your walk with Him.

We will indeed be taking a quantum leap into truth and righteousness, if we obey His command to not only love those who love us, but to love our enemies. In Matthew 5 He commanded us as follows:

You have heard that it was said, "Love your neighbour and hate your enemy." But I tell you, love your enemies and pray for those who persecute you, that you may be children of your Father in heaven. He causes his sun to rise on the evil and the good, and sends rain on the righteous and the unrighteous. If you love those who love you, what reward will you get? Are not even the tax collectors doing that? And if you greet only your own people, what are you doing more than others? Do not even pagans do that? Be perfect, therefore, as your heavenly Father is perfect.

This is intense, one might admit, but that is the command from above, and it takes God to give us the change of heart we require, to carry this through. This is where the potent power of prayer comes into play – as discussed fully in chapter seven below.

I couldn't do this by my might and power, but by the Spirit of God, the Holy Spirit that is dwelling within me. Imagine being asked to be exceptionally courteous to another, who dislikes you, wishes and plans nothing, but evil for you? The first instinct is that it will be impossible. If ever possible, how do I go about it?

Over the years, I have come to realise how simple it is – though as a mere mortal, I still fall short in this aspect. Having said that, we can start by taking a mental account of Jesus Christ's walk on earth. He was without sin, yet He died on the cross for your sins and mine. He laid down His life so you and I could be saved. The lyrics of a song that I know (by Ellis J. Crum) "He Paid a debt He Did Not Owe" sheds enormous light on this command.

He paid a debt He did not owe;

I owed a debt I could not pay;

I needed someone to wash my sins away.

And, now, I sing a brand new song,

"Amazing Grace."

Christ Jesus paid a debt that I could never pay.

He paid that debt at Calvary.

He cleansed my soul and set me free.

I'm glad that Jesus did all my sins erase.

I, now, can sing a brand new song,

"Amazing Grace."

Christ Jesus paid a debt that I could never pay.

One day He's coming back for me

To live with Him eternally.

Won't it be glory to see Him on that day!

I, then, will sing a brand new song,

"Amazing Grace."

Christ Jesus paid a debt that I could never pay.

Yes, Jesus paid a debt that I could never pay.

The benefits of loving those who love us are minimal, because even those not walking the walk practise that, but we will be truly living love for God, if we can demonstrate and extend our selfless sacrificial love, to our enemies who revile and scorn us. God did not give up on us whilst we were likewise, but endured us; hence we have no reasonable excuse to do otherwise. In the passage above, we are given guidelines on how to go about achieving fulfilment. We are to love our enemies, pray for our enemies and be perfect.

Love our enemies:

The command is, to sincerely and genuinely love our enemies. This refers to, the sort of sacrificial love, of going the extra mile, to ensure that the enemy becomes a better person. Anything short of this will not do. Mere pretence and courteousness to our enemies and not being open will not suffice. For God sees the hearts of all, and reads the intentions of it. Though it may be incomprehensible to the mortal mind, God understands our every move. It is agreeably not easy to love your enemy, but if we concentrate on Jesus' love for us, and do to others, as we would have them do to us, then we will find that, with a defined purpose-driven calculated effort, seeking to love them as completely as God loves us, and forgiving them, becomes second nature. Remember we are loving them for God!

Pray for our enemies:

When we pray, we do so in truth and in spirit, with a sincere heart and expectation of our requests being granted. So also, when we pray for our enemies, we must so do. We pray spontaneously in such a manner as to touch our enemies. Although the enemy may have knocked us down, with fervent prayers, we will knock the enemy out, and thereby, disarm him or her. We can pray, so that God gives the enemy a deep spiritual understanding, leading to the knowledge of the word and God Himself. When we do this, we will be interceding on behalf of the enemy, for God to help the enemy walk the walk, giving him or her strength and endurance.

Whatever the problem we are experiencing with our enemies, we must spell it out, in sheer simplicity, in a report to God. The manifestation of changes in our enemies' lives, as a result of our constant and ceaseless prayers, shall be counted joy in our walk. So then, faithful walkers, do not give up; but rather get going with your fervent prayers! For the effectual fervent prayer of the righteous avails much. Trust me, by loving and praying for our enemies, we can overcome evil with good to God's glory through Jesus Christ, our Lord and Saviour. Amen!

Be perfect:

The call to perfection is not to be construed as being hyperbole, for we are called to strive to be perfect in character, in holiness, in maturity and in love. In other words, in our walk, we must aspire as much as possible, to be like our Maker, with whom we are walking. We are to separate ourselves, from the world's sinful values and be totally and wholly devoted to God's desires, rather than our own selfish desires. Spiritually, we must grow in maturity to achieve Christlike nature, and wholeness in holy living, at the pace of our spiritual growth. Whatever we do, we must be determined to develop, in accordance with scripture, which says *"When I was a child, I talked like a child; I thought like a child, I reasoned like a child. When I became a man, I put childish ways behind me"* (1 Cor. 13:11).

Strive to do the right things and excel, rising above mediocrity. To do this, ask God to bless you with the spirit of wisdom, understanding and discernment, to be able to discern right from wrong, and good from bad. We are not to repay evil with evil, but be careful to do what is right in the eyes of everybody. For the word of God said "if possible, as far as it depends on you, live at peace with everyone."

On the contrary, if your enemy is hungry, feed him, if he is thirsty give him something to drink, in doing this you will heap burning coals on his head" (Rom. 12:17-20). The antidote to getting rid of your enemy is, turning him or her into a friend. Start this application now and enjoy its benefits to the glory of God. Praise His holy name for this magnificent revelation.

Striving to put God's desires above ours, and concentrating on walking in His precepts, whilst wilfully putting aside worldly desires, with a mindset of living His love, is a step in the right direction.

By obeying the command to *love your enemies and pray for those who persecute you,* we will not be overcome with evil, but become sons of God and acclaimed walkers with Him - all thanks to His grace through the redemption that came by Christ Jesus. Let us pause for a moment and praise God, who ministers to us every second of the day and bless His holy name. Praise God and His wonderful gift of Life – Jesus Christ, for His love and mercy endure forever. Hallelujah!

Will you turn over the page with me, to continue to express our gratitude with a grateful heart?

SIX

HEART OF GRATITUDE

I will praise you, O LORD, with all my heart; before the
"gods" I will sing your praise. I will bow down toward
your holy temple and will praise your name for your love
and your faithfulness, for you have exalted above all things
your name and your word. When I called, you answered
me; you made me bold and stout hearted. Ps. 138:1-3

o God be the glory, great things He has done, so loved
He the world that He gave us His Son, who yielded
His life an atonement for sin, and opened the life gate that
all may go in - justification for us to walk the walk with God.
Having learned to be bold and courageous in taking the first
step of the walk of righteousness, and resolved to come off

our high horses, to embrace the Word of God, while adopting it in our daily lives, and living it by the show of love of God and to others, what is left for us to do now, is to say a big "THANK YOU," Father God, for coming to my rescue to show me the way to eternal life. More often than not, we forget to show our appreciation to both God and mankind, and tend to leave it to others to do on our behalf. But as you will see in the book of Leviticus 7, God requires us to personally show our gratitude and, if bringing a token of our appreciation, to do it with our own hands and *never* through a medium. Talking about it is not enough. What is honourable and commendable, is a developed attitude of gratitude in our walk. As with all aspects of the walk, we must sincerely mean it, when we express our thankfulness to God and others from the bottom of our hearts.

We are blessed, not out of our own good deeds, but as a result of God's grace. Now grace is the free and unmerited favour of God, shown towards us, or better still, the divine assistance given to us, in spiritual rebirth. For it is by grace that we have been saved through faith - and this is not from ourselves nor by our works - but the gift of God so that no one can boast (Eph. 2:8). Why then do we find it hard to give thanks to God? Ordinarily when someone gives us a present, we say "thank you, but you shouldn't have" because we know we do not deserve it. What do we do in the end? We take it and keep it anyway. How much more obligated should we feel for receiving the gift of salvation from God?

The Psalmist in Psalm 95 invites us to

Come, let us sing for joy to the LORD;
let us shout aloud to the Rock of our salvation.
Let us come before Him with thanksgiving
and extol Him with music and song.
For the LORD is the great God,
the great King above all gods.
In His hand are the depths of the earth,
and the mountain peaks belong to Him.
The sea is His, for He made it,
and His hands formed the dry land.
Come, let us bow down in worship,
let us kneel before the LORD our Maker;
for He is our God
and we are the people of His pasture,
the flock under His care.
Today, if only you would hear His voice,
Do not harden your hearts as you did at Meribah,

as you did that day at Massah

in the wilderness,

where your ancestors tested me;

they tried me, though they had seen what I did.

For forty years I was angry with that generation;

I said,

"They are a people whose hearts go astray,

and they have not known my ways

So I declared on oath in my anger,

'They shall never enter my rest.'"

The obstacles standing between us and God's ultimate blessings, as we have seen in the preceding chapters, are haughty heart, disobedience, stubbornness and ungratefulness. These lead to, an ungraceful walk into a ditch, designed by our sinful overindulgence, culminating in self-destruction and condemnation. In order to avoid this happening, today, if you hear His voice, do not harden your heart, rather receive Him, and bow down in worship of Him, with thanksgiving. It is indeed good to praise God and make music to His name, proclaiming His love in the morning and His faithfulness at night for material and spiritual blessings, and for answering our prayers. We cannot afford to take God for granted in our walk with Him. This brings to mind the story of the ten lepers that were healed by Jesus Christ and likewise the parable He told of the king's ten servants in the book of Luke 17 and 19 respectively.

Story of the Ten Lepers

Leprosy is a chronic infectious disease, characterised by the formation of painful inflamed nodules beneath the skin, disfigurement and wasting of affected areas. Because of its infectious nature, people with the disease, were therefore isolated from others, and if they had to come in close contact, they were required to inform others of their disease.

Now ten men, with such a disease, called out to Jesus Christ, as He was going into a village, to have pity on them and heal them. Jesus Christ sent them away, to go show themselves to the priests. The ten lepers faithfully obeyed the command, and were healed on their way to the priests. One of the ten lepers, a Samaritan, came back praising God, in a loud voice, when he realised he was healed and, threw himself at Jesus' feet and thanked Him. Jesus then asked, "Were not all ten cleansed? Where are the other nine? Was no one found, to return to give praise to God, except this foreigner?"

Sadly, the other nine's ungrateful attitude, mirror the state of the world we live in today, making it a norm, to receive God's blessings with an ungrateful spirit.

In walking the walk of righteousness, we do not have to behave in like manner, as though, we are without knowledge of the Word of God. Remember, we can only grow in our walk, understanding God's grace, if we cultivate a grateful attitude in spirit. It thus goes without saying that, with our appreciative responsive attitude; we would receive and learn more about God. Are we falling short in this aspect of our walk? Indeed, the good news is, we can boldly bow down, toward His holy temple and, praise His name for His love and His faithfulness, for He has exalted above all things, His name and His Word. Why? Because when we called, He answered us; and made us bold and stout hearted. So we say what a mighty God we serve!

Story of the King's Ten Servants

This parable shows us, how to express our gratitude and, more so, what to do in our walk with God, whilst awaiting the second coming of Jesus Christ – which is a definite "must happen" – because the Word of God, tells us that, Jesus Christ will come in His glory and, sit on His throne in heavenly glory, to judge the living and the dead! It was told, because the people with Jesus Christ at the time thought, the kingdom of God was going to appear at once. So then, while the people were listening to these things, Jesus Christ proceeded to tell a parable, of a certain nobleman, who went to a distant country, to have himself appointed king, and then return. Before departing, he called ten of his servants, gave them ten minas, and said to them, "Put this money to work, until I come back." In other words, invest it wisely. But his subjects hated him and sent a delegation after him, saying, "We don't want this man to be our king." He was made king anyhow and, he returned home. Upon arrival, he sent for the servants he had given the money to, in order to find out what they had gained with it. One after the other, they came in to render account. The first servant said, "Sir, your mina (i.e. money) has earned ten minas more." He got a pat on the back, and a reward to take charge of ten cities. Why? Because he had been trustworthy in a very small matter. Likewise, the second servant was rewarded with taking charge of five cities. Then another servant came and said,

"Sir, here is your mina; I have laid it away in a piece of cloth. I was afraid of you, because you are a hard man, who likes to take out what he did not put in, and reap what he did not sow." The master said to him, "I will judge you by your own words, you wicked servant. Now you knew, did you, that I was a hard man, taking out what I didn't put in, and reaping what I didn't sow? Why then didn't you put my money on deposit, so that when I came back, I could have collected it with interest?" The master ordered those standing by, to "take his mina away from him, and give it to the one who has ten minas."

We learn from the above two stories, that we therefore, have to express gratitude for whatever is given to us, and strive to make the most out of it. No gift is too small or too big. We must focus on the heart of the giver and, be thankful, because if we study the conclusion of the story, it was said that "to everyone who has, more will be given, but as for the one who has nothing, even what he has, will be taken away." Presumably, this sounds harsh, but in actual fact, it is not.

Like the master in this story, God has given us, the precious gift of eternal life, His only begotten Son, and expects us, to faithfully trust and use the benefits, to grow His kingdom, in our walk with Him.

It is worth noting at this juncture that, appreciating others, not with our lips, while talking the talk, but by our deeds, while walking the walk, reflects honour in our walk of righteousness. In 1 Peter 4:11 we are commanded

"If anyone speaks, they should do so as one who speaks the very words of God. If anyone serves, they should do so with the strength God provides, so that in all things God may be praised through Jesus Christ. To Him be the glory and the power forever and ever. Amen."

A cultivated attitude, of thanking those who bless us financially or with their time, those who bring us and our church leaders joy, whilst praising God, causes onlookers to be awed by God's power. It is interesting, to note that, this deed of appreciating them in the Lord, encourages them, to continue with their good deeds, too. Otherwise, they will never know, how much, they are appreciated. A token of our appreciation, to express our feelings for their gift, blessing, help, time, ministry, leadership and teaching, will also go a long way to show our love and support.

Giving thanks, in all things, no matter the obstacles, reproaches, feelings of frustration, trials and tribulations, or circumstances, measures the rate of progression of gait in our walk. We are commanded to give thanks in all circumstances, for this is God's will for us in Christ Jesus (1 Thess. 5:18). Do we choose when, and in what situation, to give thanks? If we do, then we are not obedient to God's command, but submitting to occurrences which inevitably, fluctuate our thankfulness, joy and prayer. As much as this may go against our natural inclinations, with conscious effort, if we are determined to rise above, whatever unpleasant situation we are faced with, or find ourselves in, and obey God's command, and are thankful, we will begin to see the situation, in a different perspective to the glory of God. This is because; God immediately takes over and gives us rest.

Our walk should therefore, reflect our praises to God through singing of hymns about Him, telling others of Him and His wonders, worshipping Him in truth and in spirit, giving Him glory with our obedient deeds, bringing Him love offerings and living holy lives, no matter the circumstances.

Believe you me, I have learned in my walk, to always give thanks to God and the creation for everything, whether significant or insignificant, because I am constantly and consciously reminded that, this is His will for me, in Christ Jesus. Let me share my daily routine of thankfulness with you. I give Him thanks for every food or meal I take in, and thank Him each morning I rise from bed, before my foot touches the floor, for His protection throughout the night, whilst my family and I were sleeping. Also, before setting out of my house, I thank Him, for shielding our going out and our coming in, for covering us with the blood of Jesus Christ, for not permitting the eyes of the enemy to see any one of us, and finally thank Him for all that He has done and, those things He is doing and, about to do in our lives, because as for me and my household, we want to experience the most of our spiritual walk with Him, and all that He has in store for us for the day.

Surely, you too, have a lot to thank Him for. If you are feeling sorry for yourself, thinking you do not have anything to thank Him for, because He doesn't seem to have done much for you, or answered a particular prayer request, or it may be that presently, in your life, things are not going the way you wish them to, I challenge you to begin counting your blessings - those goodies of the past- name them if you may, and you will be surprised to note, what God has done.

There is so much He has done for us, and yet, there is so much He is about to do. Like David, in psalm 103, let us

together, take in the list of God's glorious deeds in our lives
and focus on our praises to Him accordingly.

Praise the LORD, my soul;

all my inmost being, praise His holy name.

Praise the LORD, my soul,

and forget not all His benefits —

who forgives all your sins

and heals all your diseases,

who redeems your life from the pit

and crowns you with love and compassion,

who satisfies your desires with good things

so that your youth is renewed like the eagle's.

The LORD works righteousness

and justice for all the oppressed.

He made known His ways to Moses,

His deeds to the people of Israel:

The LORD is compassionate and gracious,

slow to anger, abounding in love.

He will not always accuse,

nor will He harbour His anger forever;

He does not treat us as our sins deserve

or repay us according to our iniquities.

For as high as the heavens are above the earth,

so great is His love for those who fear Him;

as far as the east is from the west,

so far has He removed our transgressions from us.

As a father has compassion on His children,

so the LORD has compassion on those who fear Him;

for He knows how we are formed,

He remembers that we are dust.

The life of mortals is like grass,

they flourish like a flower of the field;

the wind blows over it and it is gone,

and its place remembers it no more.

But from everlasting to everlasting

the LORD's love is with those who fear Him,

and His righteousness with their children's children

with those who keep His covenant

and remember to obey His precepts.

The LORD has established His throne in heaven,

and His kingdom rules over all.

Praise the LORD, you His angels,

you mighty ones who do His bidding,

who obey His word.

Praise the LORD, all His heavenly hosts,

you His servants who do His will.

Praise the LORD, all His works

everywhere in His dominion.

Praise the LORD, my soul.

Glory to God, for there are so many of His glorious deeds, that He dishes out to us, in His good and perfect nature. We receive all these without deserving any of them. Therefore, no matter how difficult our walk is with Him, we definitely can count our blessings of the past, present and future. King David, a prophet in the Bible did, so can we too!

The ball is thus in our court, to provoke His divine blessings and, to find out how, let us together read the next chapter and put our faith into action!

SEVEN

BEING IN TUNE WITH GOD

"Evening morning and noon, I cry out in distress and he hears my voice" Ps. 55:17

*C*all to me and, I will answer you, and tell you great and unsearchable things you do not know! The cell phone, or mobile phone number to call, in obedience to this command, is JER333 (i.e. Jer. 33:3) in prayers. Store or save this spiritual number on your phone, as a reminder, to always be prayerful, in your walk with God. You may be wondering how to call Him. The response is simple; all you need do to be in tune with God, is to steadfastly pray constantly.

Prayer is nothing more than, a personal communication or petition, especially, in the form of supplication, adoration, praise, contrition or thanksgiving, addressed to a Deity. It is the vital link, between God and us.

The key to effective prayer is twofold: **attitude** and **action**. Our attitude must be one of complete dependence, demonstrating our total reliance on God, and our action, must be reflected, in our humble invitation to God, to overwhelm us, with power and faith, in circumstances that seem impossible to us, because we know, with Him, all things are possible. Notably, we cannot overcome such occurrences, without His divine intervention, with our humanly power.

It is said that, those who trust in the Lord, are like Mount Zion, which cannot be shaken, but endures forever. As the mountains surround Jerusalem, so the Lord surrounds His people, both now and forevermore (Ps. 125:1-2). We are assured of His consistency; unlike us, God is not moved, or shaken, by the changes in our society, because He already knows these changes before they happen. Isn't it great, to know and be rest assured that, we are walking with a living God, who endures forever? Glory!

A priority on the list of "must-dos", of anyone walking the walk is, essentially prayer. It is so very imperative, to make time, to pray constantly. Finding time to pray, in our daily busy schedules, can at times prove difficult, but we must bear in mind that, spending time with God, not only nurtures our relationship with Him, but equips us, to rise above life's struggles and challenges in our walk.

The good news is, we can pray wherever we are. After all, prayer is communicating with God, so we can either pray quietly in our hearts, or say a few words out, while working or doing a chore. However, it is equally important, to set time aside, to pray, by retiring into a solitary place of your choice.

The importance of this cannot adequately be stressed, but perhaps, a recount of a few instances, when Jesus Christ Himself withdrew to lonely places and prayed, might enlighten us in our walk. Jesus Christ made time, in His busy schedule, to be alone in prayer with our Father in heaven. Jesus Christ got up very early in the morning, while it was still dark, and went off, to a solitary place, to pray (Mk. 1:35).

Again, after dismissing His disciples, to go ahead of Him, He went up to the mountainside, to pray (Mk. 6:46). One of those days Jesus Christ went out to the mountainside to pray, He spent the whole night praying to God (Lk. 6:12). Jesus said to His disciples, "Sit here while I pray." He took Peter, James and John along with Him, and He began to be deeply distressed and troubled. "My soul is overwhelmed with sorrow to the point of death," He said to them. "Stay here and keep watch" (Mk. 32-34). That is how prayerful our Lord and Saviour was. We also learn from the Word of God that, before any important thing or event in Jesus Christ's life, He took time off, to seek God's face in prayers; we too, need to adopt this lifestyle in our walk.

The word of God, equally, encourages communal praying sessions, where two or more, sincerely agree on anything and, ask in Jesus Christ's name, it will be granted by our Father in heaven. The reason being, Jesus Christ's spirit, is present and is in the midst of such, who are gathered on the very occasion.

Whatever our heart desires, if we do not ask for it, we will not get it. I recently read a book, in which, it was said, there were so many blessings in heaven for us for our benefit, but we perish, without having enjoyed the full benefits, for the simple reason that, we did not ask for them. The time is ripe in our walk with Him, to delight ourselves in Him, so that whatever our heart desires, and we ask, will be granted. We are commanded in the book of Luke 11 to ask:

"So I say to you: Ask and it will be given to you; seek and you will find; knock and the door will be opened to you.

For everyone who asks receives; the one who seeks finds; and to the one who knocks, the door will be opened.

"Which of you fathers, if your son asks for a fish, will give him a snake instead? Or if he asks for an egg, will give him a scorpion? If you then, though you are evil, know how to give good gifts to your children, how much more will your Father in heaven give the Holy Spirit to those who ask Him!"

This is an invitation to, ask God for anything and every-thing, and expect anything and everything, from Him, according to His perspective. In expecting anything, we must be ready to, embrace the fact that, what we get, may not be in harmony with our request. Considering, we may not have given thought to possible alternatives, but our God, knows what is best for us, at any given time. Remember every good and perfect gift comes from above, coming down from the Father of the heavenly lights, who does not change like shifting shadows (James 1:17). The response to our prayers may also be delayed for days, weeks, months or maybe, years; however, this should not be construed as denial. God hears our requests, and will provide for us, at

117

His own appointed time. Hence, we should not be deterred by this, and give up - by all means, no! The story of the persistent widow in the book of Luke 18:2-8, teaches us in our walk of divine honour, the necessity of patience, persistency, and perseverance, in our prayer lives. We are to, always pray and not give up.

Story of the Persistent Widow:

Now, by way of introduction to the story, it is necessary to describe the predicament of widows, in ages past. Widows, in the ancient world, were taken advantage of, or bypassed in the society, leading them to become poverty stricken and, as we are commanded, we must consider their needs, not just our own.

Very well then, in a certain town, there was a judge, who neither feared God nor cared about men. And there was a widow, in that town that, kept coming to him with a plea, "Grant me justice against my adversary." For some time, the judge refused, but he finally caved in, after saying to himself that, though he did not fear God or care about his fellow human beings, yet, for the reason that, the widow kept bothering him, he would see that, she got the justice she sought, so she would not, eventually wear him out with her coming to him. "And the Lord said, listen to what the unjust judge says; And will not God bring about justice for His chosen ones – you and I, who cry out to Him day and night? I tell you, He will see that they get justice and quickly. However, when the Son of Man comes, will He find faith on the earth?"

Praying "always" or, to be persistent in prayers, does not mean, we should pray endless, repetitive prayers, every single minute of the day, with painfully long prayers. Rather, praying always means that, we should pray continually, and be faithful, in keeping, our regular quiet times of prayer sessions; whilst constantly, bringing our daily requests to Him, in faith, that He will answer them, in our walk with Him. A well maintained good habit of prayer shows dedication to, and strengthens our relationship with God in our walk with Him.

HOW DO I PRAY?

Jesus Christ answered this question, in the book of Matthew 6:9-13, when the disciples posed a similar question to Him.

This, then, is how you should pray:

Our Father in heaven,

hallowed be your name,

your kingdom come,

your will be done,

on earth as it is in heaven.

Give us today our daily bread.

And forgive us our debts,

as we also have forgiven our debtors.

And lead us not into temptation,

but deliver us from the evil one.

You will note the Lord's Prayer starts, by acknowledging God, as our Father in heaven, the only majestic and holy one, whose name is honoured and, above all other names. The reference to His kingdom come indicates, His spiritual reign, which is, also present in Jesus Christ's authority, in those walking the Walk. We pray His perfect purpose, to be accomplished, in this world and the next, when we pray that, His will be done on earth as it is in heaven. We turn to request our own needs, by acknowledging God, as the utmost provider and sustainer of, our daily requirements – our Jehovah Jireh! We ask that, He forgives us the wrong things that we have done and, keep us away and out from the claws of evil ones' deceit, and gives us strength, to overcome it, as we have chosen to, walk His way with Him. The good news is no temptation has seized you, except what is common to man. Yet, our God is faithful; He will not let you be tempted, beyond what you can bear. For the simple reason that, He sits as a refiner, in our lives, with His eyes always looking down on us. So that when you are tempted, He will also provide a way out, so that you can stand up under it! Praise be to the Almighty God!

The Lord's Prayer thus, serves as a model and breviary of prayer – the form of a request of a child, to a father - which the father answers, in his own appointed time. We must therefore, learn to put ourselves, under God's control and, wait for Him to work His works, in His own time. Do not misconstrue the waiting time, to mean, denial.

The secret of efficacy of prayer is, when it is said in the name of Jesus Christ, because the word of God tells us that, Jesus Christ, is the only way and the truth and the life, no one comes to the Father except through Him. We may ask Him, for anything, in His name and, He will do it (John 14). If you trust Jesus Christ to take you to the Father, all the benefits of the walk will be yours.

VERY IMPORTANT NOTICE:

PRAYER REQUESTS MADE IN THE NAME OF JESUS CHRIST, EQUATE, MORE THAN ENOUGH BLESSINGS

Since the Lord has set apart the godly for Himself, He will hear us when we call to Him (Ps. 4:3). I don't know about you, but for me, this is divine assurance, for trusting Jesus Christ, for my salvation.

Remember, we can pray anywhere and anytime and, He will hear us, so long as, we do not let the extremity of our problems, cause us to doubt Him.

Our prayers may be hindered, though, when we displease God. We are instructed in the book of Timothy, to lift up our holy hands wherever we are in prayer, without anger or disputing, because these make prayer difficult. This is why, we are to reconcile with whomever we have a broken relationship, grievance or misunderstanding, before approaching the throne of glory. As mentioned earlier in the preceding chapters, our relationship with others reflects our relationship with God. Hence, we need to be right with others, loving them as we ought to do.

I have learned in my walk, to rely on the Holy Spirit when I pray, since it gives me the power I need to walk the walk. In which case, no matter how adverse the situation in which, I find myself, even if I cannot pray and call on Christ's Spirit, He answers me. My daughter has learnt this too, and has adopted it. This has now turned into our favourite method of searching for misplaced items in our household. We just call JER333 and, our feet are ordered straight to the recovery point - to God's glory. We pray daily for His guidance, when we cast our burdens unto the Lord and, dedicate all that we have and own to Him. In return, by way of, assuring us of His omnipresence, He shows us what He can do, when we truly and sincerely walk with Him.

This brings to mind, a special prayer, my family and some friends prayed some years back.

I recall the experience of starting to operate a business from my office space. I was nursing my five-month-old baby at the time, when my husband rushed home in excitement that, he had found a premise from where, we could run our respective businesses. I was whisked off to the site and, when I walked through the door and saw the open plan office, suffice to say, I was not in the least interested. However, not wanting to burst my dear husband's bubble, I pointed to the left half of the site and said, "Allocate this space to me, please," and breezed out as quickly as I came in.

A few weeks down the line, I was yet again rushed into the office space. Only this time, it was beautifully demarcated, also with some good office furniture, well laid out office rooms, with conference table and I was asked to start operating the business of my law firm. However, in as much as I was pleased with my husband, I felt the strong need to, dedicate the office entirely to God. I invited some older Christian friends, to come in and pray, over and in the office, with me. We did, and have never regretted it. Whatever God says He will do, He does. My business may not be listed on the stock market, but the reward of peace and tranquillity that I enjoy, fills my heart with praises to God.

How many of us, sincerely prayed, before leaving our respective homes today? Did you know who you were going to meet today? It is very important that, we have our quiet times with God every day before setting out of our homes. This is because; in this day and age, we do not know what sort of calamity is lurking out there. It is thus, imperative to have a direct relationship with God, through prayers. We cannot depend on our pastors, parents, elders and/or close associates, to pray for us all the time. We need to cultivate the attitude of, relying on God's counsel, to guide and shield us always. As previously mentioned, no prayer is too small or too big for God. Whatever the problem, situation, or condition that you find yourself in, rather than telling it to the Creation, who definitely, do not have much to offer, tell it to the Creator, who has *all* to offer and enjoy the many benefits of the walk with Him, in full.

WAIT NO LONGER!

And a voice from heaven said, "This is my Son, whom I love; with him I am well pleased." (Matt3:17)

$\mathcal{T}$o God be the glory for the great things He has done! Throughout the various chapters of this awe-inspiring expositional book, I have outlined the essence, requirement and benefits of walking the walk, and the crux of ridding ourselves of, filthy language in talking the talk.

The central theme and focal point of this book is, to accept the call to be saved, by confessing with your mouth that, Jesus Christ is Lord and believe in your heart that God raised Him from the dead, so you are saved. Consequently, enabling you to, begin to live the Christian life by, walking the walk of righteousness in **humility** – humbling ourselves in the sight of the Lord for Him to lift us up, **obedience** - trusting and obeying every command of the word of God, **selflessness** – experiencing joy, by allowing God to express His great love, a bond of perfection, for others through us, in **love** – experiencing peace, by loving God with all our hearts, souls and minds, **gratitude** – by being thankful for the good that God has brought us, in this life and the next and, in constant **prayers** – communing daily with God for His protection and guidance.

In the Walk of righteousness, there are no barriers. Christ is all and is, in all. He accepts all who come to trust in Him, and does not give preference to, any one particular race or nationality, as being better than the other. We are all ONE, in the sight of God, who created us in His own image. And for all that seek first, His kingdom and His righteousness, all other things will be added to them in their walk of divine honour.

Walking the walk without regular soul-searching exercise is incomplete, as it is very necessary. It is a must, to take stock of your walk, every now and again and, repent when necessary. This must be viewed as purpose-driven exercises, in order to, measure the pace of walk, to determine if, God would truly also say of us, as in the verse above, "This is my child, whom I love; with whom I am well pleased." Let us walk in a way and manner that glorifies God by demonstrating **faith**, **humility**, **compassion**, **gentleness**, **kindness**, **love** and **patience** towards each other.

After all, by confessing Christ as our Lord and Saviour, we take off the old self with its practices, and put on the new self which is, being renewed in knowledge in the true image of God.

The simple prayer appearing below will be a step in the right direction (Ps. 139:23-24):

Search me, God, and know my heart;

test me and know my anxious thoughts.

See if there is any offensive way in me,

and lead me in the way everlasting. Amen

I was invited into this supernatural covenant relationship with God and because, like many others, I accepted the invitation, and obeyed the simple instructions of the Word, I am today, reaping the benefits of uncommon and unparalleled favours in abundance, to the glory of God. It is my sincerest hope that, the various testimonies and biblical illustrated examples have, broadened your knowledge, perspective and understanding of God's uncomplicated Word, to enable you to walk, resume walking or to continue in your walk.

Are you walking the Walk?

Remember, it is never too late to make the change, for it is said *"If we confess our sins, He is faithful and just and will forgive us our sins and purify us from all unrighteousness"* (1 John 1:9). Start walking the walk now: the benefits are great!

God bless you, as you respond.

www.olawunmibiriyok.com

REMORSEFUL PRAYER
OF THE FAITHFUL
(in line with Psalm 51)

Have mercy on me, O God,

according to your unfailing love;

according to your great compassion

blot out my transgressions.

Wash away all my iniquity

and cleanse me from my sin.

For I know my transgressions,

and my sin is always before me.

Against you, you only, have I sinned

and done what is evil in your sight;

so you are right in your verdict

and justified when you judge.

Surely I was sinful at birth,

sinful from the time my mother conceived me.

Yet you desired faithfulness even in the womb;

you taught me wisdom in that secret place.

Cleanse me with hyssop, and I will be clean;

wash me, and I will be whiter than snow.

Let me hear joy and gladness;

let the bones you have crushed rejoice.

Hide your face from my sins

and blot out all my iniquity.

You do not delight in sacrifice, or I would bring it;

you do not take pleasure in burnt offerings.

My sacrifice, O God, is a broken spirit;

a broken and contrite heart

you, God, will not despise.

Create in me a pure heart, O God,

and renew a steadfast spirit within me.

Do not cast me from your presence

or take your Holy Spirit from me.

Restore to me the joy of your salvation

and grant me a willing spirit, to sustain me.

O LORD Jesus Christ, intervene and intercede on my

behalf and have my supplication

granted by my heavenly Father for I pray through your

mighty name; Amen

To God be the Glory!

I now leave you with the lyrics of Elisha Albright Hoffman

(1839-1929) song,

What a fellowship, what a joy divine,

Leaning on the everlasting arms;

What a blessedness, what a peace is mine,

Leaning on the everlasting arms.

o Refrain:

Leaning, leaning, safe and secure from all alarms;

Leaning, leaning, leaning on the everlasting arms.

Oh, how sweet to walk in this pilgrim way,

Leaning on the everlasting arms;

Oh, how bright the path grows from day to day,

Leaning on the everlasting arms.

What have I to dread, what have I to fear,

Leaning on the everlasting arms?

I have blessed peace with my Lord so near,

Leaning on the everlasting arms.

About the award-winning Author

*M*rs Olawunmi Biriyok, MIoD, FRSA, holds a BSc Degree in International Studies and LLB Hons (Lond). A Christian Lawyer and award-winning Author of inspirational books – her debut book being "Walk the Walk and stop just talking the talk" (2011). She has since released a second inspirational book "The Manual for Righteous Living", which won two 2012 Christian Literary awards. All her books and works do, indeed, inspire virtuous character and, are also a valuable addition to every Christian's devotional library.

Mrs Biriyok runs, Personal Empowerment Ministry Sessions, (PEMS) - a Christian counselling ministry – that empowers and develops a unique personal relationship with

God. Whatever spiritual assistance you require, you have the right to, and will, be treated with the love and fear of God, care and respect.

Mrs Biriyok is a good and seasoned speaker on Christian values; she has shared the Word of God in the UK, USA and Ghana.

The author is a married mother of four children, who has effectively balanced hectic professional demands, with being a positive role model, wife and mother. She has advised and assisted numerous Churches, on legal issues and currently holds a voluntary role of a Safeguarding Officer for Children and Vulnerable Adults at her local parish.

In 2001, Mrs Olawunmi Biriyok was invited to join the Solicitors Sole Practitioners Group (SPG) England and Wales in order to enjoy a relaxed atmosphere of interacting professionally with her learned colleagues. After four years of such interaction, Mrs Biriyok was elected onto the SPG Executive Committee, to contribute to its growth and positive changes, by assisting the decision-makers and/or advising her fellow Legal Practitioners.

Mrs Olawunmi Biriyok subsequently, chaired the Sole Practitioners Group of England and Wales (2010-2011) and is currently the Honorary Secretary of the South London Law Society of England and Wales.

To arrange a book signing, interview, speaking engagement or personal counselling sessions, contact Olawunmi Biriyok at, obiriyok@gmail.com, or at www.olawunmi-biriyok.com or on +44(0)7738291030 (UK) or +1832-443-0435 (USA)

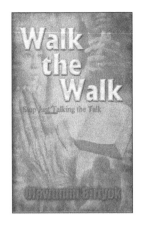

Author's Debut Book

*I*n this empowering, expositional novel, the author introduces the reader to key elements of "the walk of righteousness" such as faith, humility, compassion, obedience, selflessness, love and prayer. Mrs. Biriyok demonstrates these virtues through stories of key Biblical figures such as Noah, Abraham, and Moses in the Old Testament and Jesus Christ and the apostle Peter in the New Testament. From these stories, she draws practical lessons for the Christian of today. Throughout the book, she weaves the thread of her own life changing experiences and the practical ways she has shown her faith and compassion for others. This little book is a valuable addition to the devotional library for either the new Christian searching for guidance or the experienced Christian who seeks renewal and enlightenment in the walk of faith, providing knowledge beyond what you may gain in your regular attendance of church.

Author's Award-winning book

The Manual for Righteous Living is a refreshing game-changing source of strength to transcend the frailties and pitiful arrogance of humans in order to receive the covering, security, endless provision of Abba Father. This empowering inspirational book offers immense insight to all truth seekers. The author's challenging biblical illustrations and stories of key Biblical figures throughout the book, further expounded in analogous reference to an ordinary manual go to show extraordinary faith and lifestyle of characters of the old and the new era worthy of emulating. Mrs Biriyok introduces the reader to key elements of "the manual for righteousness" such as repentance and salvation, faith, knowledge of the word, abiding in the Word, evangelising, commitment and hope. The instructional approach to the key elements of holiness and godliness provides knowledge beyond what you may gain in your regular church attendance and provokes the quest for knowledge and closeness to God. Whilst it subtly transforms your old ways thereby birthing in you the new creature to God's glory. A valuable addition to the devotional library for either the new or the experienced Christian.

To arrange a book signing, interview, speaking engagement or personal ministry sessions, contact Olawunmi Biriyok at obiriyok@gmail.com, or at www.olawunmibiriyok.com or on +1832-443-0435 or +44 773 829 1030

Lightning Source UK Ltd.
Milton Keynes UK
UKHW040643100322
399865UK00001B/98